TABLE OF CONTENTS
INTRODUCTION

Implementation	p. 4
The Connection	p. 6
Rainbow Play Tips For Transfer	p. 7
Ice Breaker Activities	p. 8

CHAPTER 1- FROM THE INSIDE OUT! — p.10
    FEELINGS IDENTIFICATION — p.11
    ENERGY — p.14
    BREATHING — p.16

CHAPTER 2- YOGA MOVES — p.18
    MINDFUL MOVEMENT — p.19
    REPRODUCIBLE ILLUSTRATIONS — p.22

CHAPTER 3- PAY ATTENTION! — p.48
    FOCUSED AWARENESS EXERCISES — p.51

CHAPTER 4- IMAGINE! — p.55
    IMAGINARY JOURNEY WORK — p.56
    EXERCISES — p.58

CHAPTER 5- EXPRESS YOURSELF! — p.70
    CREATIVE DRAMA — p.71
    BODY AWARENESS — p.74
    MOVEMENT STORY — p.79
    VALUES AND ATTITUDES — p.81

CHAPTER 6- ENRICHMENT — p.84
    SENSORY ENHANCEMENT, COLOR, AROMATHERAPY, MUSIC — p.85
    SUBJECT BASED LESSONS — p.86
    GAMES — p.87

CHAPTER 7- STANDARDS FOR BEHAVIOR — p.88
    CONFLICT RESOLUTION — p.90
    INTEGRATION — p.91
    AFFIRMATIONS — p.93
    REPRODUCIBLES — p.94
    INFORMATION FORMS — p.130
    SUGGESTED MATERIALS — p.133
    RESOURCES — p.135

PRINTED IN THE UNITED STATES OF AMERICA. THIS PUBLICATION IS PROTECTED BY UNITED STATES COPYRIGHT. IT IS FOR THOSE TRAINED IN THE RAINBOW PLAY PROGRAM. ILLUSTRATIONS OF POSTURES AND REPRODUCIBLE WORKSHEETS MAY BE COPIED, BY A TRAINED RAINBOW PLAY FACILITATOR FOR PRE-K-12 CLASSROOM INSTRUCTION ONLY. ANY VIOLATOR MAY BE SITED FOR COPYRIGHT INFRINGEMENT.

Copyright © 2000, 2002, 2003, 2004 Rainbow Play. All rights reserved.

The amount of negative sensory input to which we are subjected has grown dramatically during the last 30 or 40 years but our children have had to absorb it without any new coping skills with which to process it. The results have been disastrous for their young minds. Repeated accounts of tragic incidents resulting in death and serious injury plague our nation's public schools but there has not been an effective solution to the problem. We have only addressed the symptoms of this dilemma rather than focus on the underlying cause.

Many factors are to blame for our children's deteriorating values. Their attention is constantly being diverted with an on going stream of information. When do they ever utilize their time for imaginative play, artistic creativity, sitting in silence and/or just relaxing and being at peace with themselves? When do they take time to get in touch with how they feel and understand their emotions? How do children learn to value and respect themselves when all society seems to value is achievement and money at the expense of our own humanity? How do they begin to have empathy and compassion for others?

To effect a change in our children, we must alter their frame of reference and give them a new perspective from which to view the world. We begin by teaching them how to cultivate personal awareness in their own lives. We teach them how to recognize their feelings and how to respond to stimuli moment to moment so that they are able to heal and project that healing outward. We must educate them about the value of life and of all living things. Self-awareness must become a part of their character. The challenge is creating the time and incorporating a method that is easily integrated into their daily curriculum.

I have developed The Rainbow Play Program, which blends educational concepts with stress management techniques, character building, and creative drama to create an atmosphere of serenity in the classroom. This program is designed to increase a child's level of self-awareness. It allows children to recognize feelings as they occur and develop the tools to respond appropriately in any situation rather than react blindly. The ability to respond effectively in a stressful situation builds self-confidence. A child who feels good about himself is able to feel good about others.

The lesson format is built around theater games and simple mindful movement exercises. This is fun but also offers a creative approach to renew energy and concentration during the day. This play break, a 21st century version of recess, will include: diaphragmatic breathing, imaginary journeywork, focused awareness exercises, and sensory enhancement. Teachers may integrate various Rainbow Play techniques as part of the daily routine to instill a sense of balance and wholeness in children.

In this program:
- A.) Students learn simple mindful movement exercises and stress management techniques.
- B.) Students write and talk about their feelings.
- C.) Teacher mirrors feelings back.
- D.) Students use mindful movement, creativity, sound and stress management techniques to get in touch with specific emotions and attendant feelings.
- E.) Students act out stories that reflect their feelings using movement and stress management techniques to explore emotions.

Our children's inability to respond effectively under pressure has resulted in hostile school environments. This is a complex problem. The Rainbow Play Program is not a quick fix solution. It is a process to invoke change. Rainbow Play is an innovative approach incorporating techniques that stimulate both intrapersonal and interpersonal development. It teaches children how to connect with themselves and others. Rainbow Play goes beyond verbal communication skills enabling children to utilize other forms of expression. It combines a unique blend of methods, which foster a child's capacity to cultivate character traits such as personal awareness, confidence, empowerment, empathy, compassion, respect, and cooperation. Children will realize that when faced with a difficult situation they can draw on internal strengths to respond appropriately rather than react blindly. Thus, leading to a decrease in aggressive behavior.

My hope for the future is that over time students will be able to help themselves respond effectively under stressful circumstances rather than resort to acts of violence. A commitment to our children's social, emotional, mental, behavioral, and physical well-being is essential to their progression into healthy adulthood. Together we can make a difference in their lives. Use this program with honor, love, and compassion for the sake of our children's posterity.

IMPLEMENTATION

This book is a guide for daily implementation. The teacher will introduce each part of the program with a basic lesson. Teacher directed activity for basic outlined lessons would be between 20 and 40 minutes in length. How a teacher manages the program during the course of the day, once the basics have been taught to students, will vary. As a consideration for the importance of schedule and school structure, the program allows for flexibility of time and space, which also makes this program easily, adapted to a variety of settings. Please note that some lessons contain variations for students at the pre-school level. It is suggested you review the book in its entirety before implementing lessons. See Chapter 6 for examples of how a teacher might integrate Rainbow Play into the day.

Rainbow Play School Model For Implementation:

<u>Rainbow Play Cooperative Discipline and Suggestions for Establishing Classroom Rules</u> are put into effect the 1st week of school.

<u>Diaphragmatic Breathing</u> - Taught by all teachers the 1st two weeks of school. Check children over several weeks to make sure they are breathing correctly.

<u>Mindful Movement</u> - One posture taught each day. Each consecutive day review the previous days posture. Continue until all postures are learned. All postures and breathing should be demonstrated and practiced within in the 1st six weeks of school. The whole school will devote the first 10 - 20 minutes of the school day, breathing and practicing mindful movement exercises through out the school year.

<u>Feelings Identification</u> - Initial lesson taught within the 1st month of school. After the initial lesson, Feelings Identification activities may be taught weekly or bi weekly throughout several months or over the course of a year.

Values and Attitudes - May be taught within the 1st month along with Feelings Identification or it may be taught as a separate entity as children become more adept at expressing themselves. The teacher may use her own judgment as when to introduce this lesson. It may be taught monthly or bi-weekly based on the 10 Steps for Getting Along With Others.

Focused Awareness - Initial lesson taught in the 3rd month. Activities may be done daily, weekly, or monthly through out the year.

Imaginary Journey Exercises - Initial lesson taught in the 4th month. Activities may be done daily, weekly, or monthly through out the year.

Creative Drama - These lessons may be taught after the first 6 weeks or within the first 4 months. These activities may be used daily, weekly, or monthly.

Creative Movement - Stories should be introduced after mindful movement postures have been practiced for about 2 - 4 months. Students should be able to name and recognize a posture and be able to connect feelings with postures before students and teachers attempt to create movement stories.

Conflict Resolution - Exercise should be taught and procedures for implementing the exercise should be established in the 1st 4 months.

Sensory Enhancement - May be used through out year depending on teacher's comfort level.
All teachers, administrators, and staff should be trained in the Rainbow Play Program. Classroom teachers may choose to teach all lessons and activities or coordinate activities with special teachers. Administrators and staff should integrate RP as part of their school management program. For example, the Gym teacher may work with breathing, mindful movement, body awareness and focused awareness activities. The Music teacher may work with Focused Awareness activities. The Art teacher may work with Imaginary Journey Work combined with art. Imaginary journeys may have a theme. Artwork based on the theme is created through these journeys. For example, World Peace, Nature, Body/Mind Connection. Drama Teacher or Media Specialist may work with Creative Movement stories. All teachers work with Standards for Behavior and Values and Attitudes.

THE CONNECTION

HOW DO THE TECHNIQUES LEARNED IN THE RAINBOW PLAY PROGRAM TRANSFER TO DAILY LIVING?

The school environment should promote social life. To that end Rainbow Play has been designed as a comprehensive multidisciplinary approach. It fosters the nurturing of children not only in school but in their homes and communities as well!

School personnel are encouraged to model techniques daily. The techniques include Feelings Identification, Diaphragmatic Breathing, Mindful Movement as creative expression, Focused Awareness Exercises, Imaginative Journey Work, Creative Arts, and Sensory Enhancement. When these techniques are practiced regularly, children learn to integrate them as strategies for living and are better equipped to cope in the face of adversity.

How do these techniques transfer into strategies for living?
1. Be conscious of body signals.
2. Breathe to calm my mind and body.
3. Stay focused in the moment and allow my mind to be flexible.
4. Concentrate and relax.
5. Express myself effectively and in the most socially acceptable manner for the situation.
6. Manage myself and make well thought choices.

What are we learning?
1. Social Competence (Interpersonal skills).
2. How to create a positive, calm environment.
3. How to establish standards for behavior (Respect is the only necessary rule).
4. Character building strategies.
5. How to establish rules and regulations for responding to violence.

What are the benefits?
1. Decrease in disciplinary action.
2. Enhanced degree of calmness equals a decrease in aggressive and violent behavior.
3. Increase in participation.
4. Increase in concentration, which equals improved academic achievement.

What are the program goals?
1. To have children utilize diaphragmatic breathing as a tool to calm down and relax.
2. To give children tools for listening to their bodies and becoming aware of how the mind and body are connected.
3. To have children use mindful movement to learn how to focus their mind.
4. To give children tools so they are able to identify their feelings and think clearly.
5. To utilize the creative process to help children express and process feelings.

RAINBOW PLAY TIPS FOR TRANSFER (Reinforce during lessons)

The observation forms in the back of the book may be given as a qualitative assessment at the beginning, middle and/or end of the year as a way to see how use of the program effects behavior and academic progress. The teacher may remind children at the start of the day to use various techniques and ask at the end of the day how many remembered to use those same techniques.

How do we help students make the connection? Remind them everyday, before school begins and at the end of the day before they go home. Example: *Remember to use your breathing today* or *How many used their breathing today?* Refer to body signals.
Example: *When you are angry how do you feel inside?* Answers: heart pounds, blood races, shaky, etc.
How do you behave? Answers: Pout, yell, stomp my feet.
What thoughts go through your mind? Answer: I hate so and so.
What do you need to do so you can think clearly? Answer: breathe
How will breathing help you? Answer: Calm down so I won't hurt myself or someone else.
When is a good time to stop and pay attention to body signals? When you are confused about how you feel. When you think you are angry or very excited.
When is a good time to use diaphragmatic breathing? When a child feels angry, sad or over stimulated. For Example, after lunch, in a time out or before speaking to someone when they are angry.
What does taking time to breathe allow you to do? Calm down, focus, think, and make a choice about how to respond rather than automatically reacting.
How does practicing mindful movement exercises help you? Mindful movement exercises help you to respect and honor your body. Practicing helps you understand how your thoughts and actions are connected. Practicing mindful movement everyday may help you become aware of what you are doing while you do it.

How do Focused Awareness Exercises relate to every day? Practicing these exercises help children to become better able to bring their attention back to a task after their mind wonders. For example, if they are doing their homework and they start to wonder they can use a symbol like a stop sign or the word "Stop" to bring them back to the task. The exercises, train them to focus their attention when they need to monitor themselves.

How can students use imaginary journeys on their own? Let students know that they can make up their own journeys when they need to relax or gather their thoughts. A good time might be when they are trying to fall asleep at night or if they need to get away from a stressful situation like parents arguing. Imaginary Journey Work is a good tool for grounding students. Grounding is a technique used to balance the mind and body when a child feels scattered. It heightens a student's ability to feel from within himself.

A good exercise to help them understand how to use the techniques they are learning is to allow them an opportunity to write about a situation involving a specific feeling. Ask them to write all the details, including what body signals helped them to understand what they felt and what Rainbow Play activity they would use to help them manage their feelings and/or behavior if they found themselves in that situation again.

ICE BREAKER ACTIVITIES

When working with a group of students for the 1st time, it is fun to play introduction games to ease tension and inhibitions. Young children need help with spatial boundaries. Use a beanbag placed on the floor to keep children adequately spaced. Review the following activities for age appropriateness of your group.

The Bean Bag - Name Game - Have children sit in a wide circle. Place beanbags, mats on the floor to keep children adequately spaced. The teacher throws a beanbag to a student. The students stand up, say their name in a strong, clear voice, sit down, and throw the beanbag back to the teacher. The teacher continues this activity till all students have had a turn. You may also pass the beanbag in a circle from child to child. Child stands up, says their name, all the other students repeat their name, and the child sits down and passes it to the next child.
Variation: Give children a beanbag or a bandana and instruct them to use it in different ways (put your bean bag on your shoulder, under your chin, etc).

Blow up Balloons and give each child a balloon. Have each child try to keep his/her balloon from touching the floor. Play music in the background and play for about 3 minutes. Spread beanbags on the floor and suggest children try to stay close to their beanbag. This will keep young children from bumping into each other.
Variation: Have children keep balloons up in the air using different body parts or working with a partner.

Name body parts for children to touch or move – "Touch your nose." "Move your arm." Instruct children to touch one body part to another (hand to foot, for example). Then, suggest they touch body parts to other body parts that you know are impossible. This teaches that some body parts have limitations (head to stomach, for example).

READ THE STORY - <u>FROM HEAD TO TOE</u> BY ERIC CARLE - Allow children to act out activities while reading the story.

Tension/Release Song – The tension release song is a good beginning exercise to help students ease inhibitions. Use it at the beginning of a mindful movement session. It is a great way to foster self-esteem and to work out tension. Sing this song to the tune of "Skid a marink a doo".

Head and shoulders, knees and toes, head and shoulders, knees and toes, I love you.
(Touch body parts and wrap your arms around your self on I love you.)

Repeat

I love my back and bottom, my hair is special too!
(Touch body parts open palm)

I love my chest and belly, I'm special through and through - Oh
(Touch body parts and run hands up and down entire body)

Head and shoulders, knees and toes, head and shoulders, knees and toes,
I....Love.....You! I really do!

(Touch body parts and give yourself a hug)

Shake or Dance your Sillies Out –Tell children to Hang Like a Rag doll, have them slowly come to standing then let them shake their sillies our or dance to music. Use Instruments - Hand out instruments and let children make noise (play music).
Variation: Play music, allow children to dance, when the music stop children freeze in a silly position. Continue in this fashion for 5 minutes.

Circle Time – While children sit in a circle, have them stand, say their name, and do their favorite pose.

Partners - Have children get into partners and tell each 2 things about themselves. For example, favorite color and favorite animal. Have children listen to your directions to attach different body parts, for example put your legs together or put your arms together, etc.

When I Go To California – Sit in Circle. 1st person says, When I go to California, I'm going to take a _____(any object). This continues around the circle. Each player takes in exact order, all that has gone before and adds a new object. At the end the whole group in unison repeats the entire verse.

Mirroring – Break into partners. One of the pair becomes A, the other B. All pairs play simultaneously. A faces B. Explain that B is a person looking in a mirror. A is the persons image in the mirror. A reflects all movements initiated by B. After a minute, teacher calls for position to be reversed.

Hot Potato – Players sit in circle. One person begins holding a beanbag. The players pass the beanbag. Teacher plays music. Teacher randomly stops music. The player holding the beanbag when the music stops is out. This continues until there is one person left holding the beanbag.

DOG AND BONE – All players sit in circle except for one. The dog sits in the
middle with a "bone" within arms reach. Eyes are closed. One player (the master) signals another player to steal the bone. If the players can get the bone without being heard by the dog, he becomes the dog; if not, the dog continues until the bone is successfully stolen. If the dog hears the thief, he points in direction of the noise, if the dog is correct, the thief returns to his place and another thief is chosen.

Games in the back of the book may also be used as ice breakers or closing activities.

Some suggested CD's are:
ALL TIME FAVORITE DANCES, KIMBO EDUCATIONAL
TODDLERS SING ROCK - N- ROLL, MUSIC FOR LITTLE PEOPLE
ROCK 'N ROLL FITNESS FUN, KIMBO EDUCATIONAL
FANTASY KIDS CLASSICS, EMI RECORDS Ltd.

CHAPTER 1

FROM THE INSIDE OUT!

FEELINGS IDENTIFICATION

Feelings may be described as an emotional awareness or consciousness. Healthy expression of our feelings is essential for physical and emotional well-being. When we teach children how to recognize and identify their feelings, we give them the primary tools necessary for understanding themselves and others. By helping children explore their feelings they become able to connect emotions with events and recognize emotional messages conveyed in language. Feelings are in integral part of the human experience. For mature, meaningful relationships to develop children must be able to voice emotions and behave in socially acceptable ways to get their needs met.

ANTICIPATORY SET
FOCUS - Feelings
PURPOSE - To explore feelings.
MOTIVATION - Read a book about feelings. Suggestion - A to Z Do you Ever Feel Like Me? By Bonnie Hausman (See Suggested Materials for other titles).
TRANSFER - How do you know what you are feeling? Do you notice a change in your body? Do you notice a change in your thoughts? Do you know what you are feeling right now?
3 SIGNALS TO HELP KNOW WHAT YOU ARE FEELING For example, *When I'm getting ready to go on a special trip, I smile a lot.* (Outer Body Signals or Body Language) - *My thoughts race from one thing to the next.* (Thought Signals or Mental energy) *My body feels full of energy, like the fizz in a can of pop, it wants to move around* (Inner Body Signals or Physical Clues). *These body signals let me know I feel excited.*

OBJECTIVE
The student will connect body signals with feelings.
The student will recognize and name feelings.

INPUT & MODELING
1. Motivational activity
2. Explain to students that the whole class is going to play a game. To play this game they have to use their imagination because everybody is going to pretend that everything you say is real.
3. Explain that each time you describe an imaginary event, you want them to pay attention to the signals in their body that help them know how they feel. Each time you pause during the story, this is their cue to think about how they feel and what changes in their body let them know what they are feeling.

CHECK FOR UNDERSTANDING
4. Ask students if they have any questions.
5. Answer all questions.
6. Ask them if they are ready to play.

GUIDED PRACTICE
7. Begin telling them a story. Alter the story to fit your particular needs. Sample Teacher Script: Ok, boys and girls instead of having afternoon classes today we are going to the park to play. (Pause for reflection) When we get there, keep your eyes open. I need you to look for a big white truck and listen for a bell. The driver inside the truck rings the bell to signal he is coming. The person in that truck is the ice cream man. I am going to treat you all to ice cream. (Pause for reflection) We can sit down under the trees by the pond to eat our ice cream. The grass is soft and we can watch the ducks swim. The sun is out today and there is a light breeze. I can't think of a better way to enjoy our ice cream.

(Pause for reflection) Unfortunately, the playground is being renovated so we can't play on the swings or the slide. Even the monkey bars are closed today. (Pause for Reflection) Since we will be walking to and from the park our little trip should take most of the afternoon. Therefore, when we get back, I'll probably only have enough time to read a story and then it will be time to go home. (Pause for Reflection)

CLOSURE
8. How many of you notice the connection between the physical sensations in your body and your feelings? I would like you to begin paying attention to the changes in your body in different situations and the feelings that arise at those times.

EXTENSION
Use various Rainbow Play techniques to balance yourself. For example, if you are feeling angry, use relaxation breathing to help you focus and calm down. If you are nervous about an upcoming event or situation use imaginary journeywork to help you center yourself.

INDEPENDENT PRACTICE
9. Record your feelings and the body changes that coincide with those feelings in your journal. Do this everyday for a week.
10. Beginning next week, we will have a feeling word for each week. (Refer to Chapter 7) Younger students may need adult supervision or you may wish to facilitate assignment in classroom) You will receive a worksheet with the feeling word. Think of an instance during the week when you felt like the word of the week. Draw a picture of yourself that shows the changes that took place in your body to help you recognize what you felt. You may also write a sentence to describe the picture. Worksheet will be due the following Monday.
11. Teacher may choose to have students' pair up and share, get in groups and share, or briefly observe each students individual work. This does not need to take more then 5 minutes. If you choose, you may collect them and comment.

Variations For Pre-School Students:
MOTIVATION - Read a book about feelings. Suggestion - Today I Feel Silly and other Moods That Make My Day by Jamie Lee Curtis (See Suggested Materials for other titles).

INPUT & MODELING
1. Motivational activity
2. The teacher will show students a picture of a happy face. She will ask students to describe the emotion they see in the picture.
3. After the children have identified the emotion, the teacher will ask students to tell about a time when they felt this way. Example: I felt happy when … .
4. Explain to students that the whole class is going to play a game. To play this game they have to use their imagination because everybody is going to pretend that everything you say is real.
5. Explain that each time you describe an imaginary event, you want them to pay attention to the signals in their body that help them know how they feel. Each time you pause during the story, this is their cue to think about how they feel and what changes in their body let them know what they are feeling. This can be done quietly while children sit with eyes closed or everybody can pantomime together (this method suggested when working with children under the age of 6). Explain to children that Pantomime is when you act with your body and facial expression but not with word. Model for them by showing them how you would look if you were surprised, sad, or lonely. Have them try a few expressions.

EXTENSION

Have children color faces (refer to worksheet in appendix) and paste them back to back on a tongue depressor. Tell them a story and have them raise the correct face to explain how they feel. Use the story above with the feelings happy and sad or joyful and sad. You will probably only want to use two feelings at a time. Explain to students how they can use various Rainbow Play techniques to balance themselves. For example, if you are feeling angry, use relaxation breathing to help you focus and calm down. If you are nervous about an upcoming event or situation use imaginary journeywork to help you center yourself.

INDEPENDENT PRACTICE

10. Each week focus on a feeling word. (Refer to Reproducibles for worksheet. Students will need adult supervision or you may wish to facilitate assignment in classroom) you will receive a worksheet with the feeling word. Think of an instance during the week when you felt like the word of the week. Draw a picture of yourself that shows the changes that took place in your body to help you recognize what you felt.
11. Teacher may choose to have students bring work to next session and briefly observe each student's individual work or share as a group.

ENERGY

FOCUS - Energy
PURPOSE – To connect feelings and the bodies energy
MOTIVATION – Help children relate 4 different energy types with things in their environment. Ask," What are some things that float?" Answers: a leaf falling from a tree, bubbles, balloon, etc.... What are some things that pop? Popcorn, a balloon, etc.... What are some things that shake? A rattle, a tambourine, etc.... What are some things that are stiff? A stick, a slide, etc....
TRANSFER – Have you ever felt shaky like a rattle or stiff like a board? What do you think causes our body to feel different at different times? Answer: The energy in our body changes form. What is energy? Activity forces or power. Sometimes energy in our body changes because our feelings about things change and effects how our body reacts. Some changes don't feel as good as others. Something that effects how the energy in our body changes is stress. Who knows what stress is? When our body feels strained, mental, or physical pressure. When energy in our body changes because of our feelings, we have the ability to control that energy through the use of Rainbow Play tools.

OBJECTIVE
The student will connect feelings and the way the body reacts in relation to how the energy in our body changes when our feelings change.
The student will understand how energy in the body may be channeled into another form.

INPUT & MODELING
1. Either model with your own body or show students various types of energy.
2. Toss a balloon in the air and watch it float down. Have children state the energy type. Bring in a trouble game and press the popping device. Have children state the energy. Bring in a piece of wood and have children state the energy type. Shake a rattle and have children state the energy type. Any object may be used to model the various energies. You may also model this energy with your arm and ask children to state the energy.
3. Explain to students that they will create this energy with their own body. Tell them that you will instruct them on what energy to imitate and what body part to use. This exercise can be done with the whole body or using a body part like an arm or leg.

CHECK FOR UNDERSTANDING
4. Ask students if they have any questions about what you will be doing as a class.
5. Answer all questions.

GUIDED PRACTICE
6. Instruct students to either lie or sit still.
7. Ask them to pop their arm up and then slowly release it down.
8. Ask them to float their arm up and then slowly float it down.
9. Ask them to shake their arm and then stop.
10. Ask them to make their arm stiff and then loose.
11. Once the group has changed the energy in a body part, if space permits, use music that exudes the various energies and have children use their whole body to convey the energy type.
12. Discuss with students how the inside of our body sometimes changes energy the same way we made our arm change energy. For example, when we are nervous sometimes it feels like our body is quivering like Jell-O or our heart is popping like popcorn. Sometimes when we are scared we feel frozen or stiff like we can't move. Discuss various examples. Talk with children about our ability to changes the

energy in our body by changing the way we breathe or focusing on something specific like an imaginary journey or a particular action. Let students know that we will learn more about these different tools to help us change our energy.

CLOSURE
13. What is energy? What is stress? What are some reasons the energy in our body changes.

EXTENSION
Give children incentives to utilize Rainbow Play tools to change the energy in their body. For example, remind children to use their breathing when they are angry with another student or when they are in a time out. Give their cooperative discipline team points (see Chapter 7) when you notice them using the tool.

INDEPENDENT PRACTICE
Set up a corner of the room with books on the topics of feelings and energy.

BREATHING

Bringing our attention to the breath at any given moment allows one to be calm and more aware. When we focus our attention on our breathing, we are able to tune into how we feel in the present moment, bringing clarity and stability to our minds. When students understand diaphragmatic breathing they may use it while practicing other stress management techniques. Diaphragmatic breathing is a good tool for relaxation. It enables students to see clearly and act from a peaceful center creating a state of inner balance. The following lesson may be used to instruct children how to breathe using the diaphragm.

ANTICIPATORY SET
FOCUS - Diaphragmatic Breathing (Relaxation Breathing)
PURPOSE - To use breathing as a technique for calming inner energy.
MOTIVATION - Slowly blow up a balloon and slowly let the air out. Ask students what part of their body is like a balloon. Discuss.
TRANSFER - Explain that you will show them a way of breathing that will help them to relax. They will imagine a balloon in their body between their belly and their chest. This is where the diaphragm (a partition of muscles and tendons) is located. The opening of the balloon is by their belly. The other end of the balloon is by their chest.

OBJECTIVE
The student will understand and be able to use diaphragmatic breathing as a tool to bring clarity and stability to his mind.

INPUT & MODELING
1. Motivational Activity. Teacher will have students sit in a circle. She will lie in the middle of the circle (or use a child who has previously learned the technique) and place a small object (book) or her own hand on her diaphragm (between chest and belly). She may also choose to pair up with another student and place their head on her diaphragm.
3. She will explain the technique as she models. (Suggestion - Prepare an audio tape to guide you through the exercise.)
4. Slowly count to three or five. Breathing in through the nose, the diaphragm should expand while raising the object. Slowly reverse the count. Release breath through mouth. Diaphragm should go flat. Variation - Standing - Hand on diaphragm - hand moves forward and backward as student breathes. Sitting - Hand on diaphragm - hand moves forward and backward as student breathes. Eventually, students will inhale and exhale through nose.

CHECK FOR UNDERSTANDING
5. After the demonstration, teacher asks students if they have any questions about the breathing exercise.
6. Teacher answers all questions.

GUIDED PRACTICE
7. Teacher asks all students to take the position she has chosen for the exercise.
8. She makes sure all students have the object they will use as a visual confirmation for breathing correctly.
9. Teacher guides students through the Relaxation Breathing exercise. If space permits, students will lie on the floor. Students place a small object (book) or own hand on their diaphragm (between chest and

belly) or pair up with another student and place heads on the diaphragm. Breathing in through nose, on the count of five, the diaphragm should expand while raising the object. Slowly reverse the count and release breath through your mouth. Diaphragm should go flat. (When students are ready they will inhale and exhale through their nose.) Standing - Hand on diaphragm - hand moves forward and backward as student breathes. Plan time according to student's age. Very young children will not be able to do this for long without becoming distracted. Start at 30 seconds work up to 5 minutes depending on age.

CLOSURE
10. Discuss how students feel or have them journal about it. (See Chapter 7)

INDEPENDENT PRACTICE
You may suggest students try this technique when they are being disciplined in a time out or before beginning something they are nervous about doing.

EXTENSION
Count inhalations and exhalations as a focused awareness exercise.
Variations For Pre-School Students:

CLOSURE
Discuss how students feel – write a classroom journal entry. (See Chapter 7)

EXTENSION
After children have been using the breathing for a few weeks, you may show them a pink heart cut from construction paper. Tell them while they are breathing to imagine the pink heart in place of their own heart inside their body. Tell them to think about how it feels when someone they love is holding and hugging them. Tell them they can think about these feelings whenever they use their breathing. It is good for them to associate those kinds of feelings with relaxation breathing.

CHAPTER 2

YOGA MOVES

MINDFUL MOVEMENT

The mind and body work together to build concentration, flexibility, strength, and balance. When students practice mindful movement, paying attention to their breath and the physical sensations experienced, they build a strong foundation because it allows them to see and feel themselves in a new way. They learn body awareness which enables them to think more clearly so that they respond rather then react to stimuli. When they use their mind to imagine, imitate, and focus, they learn flexibility of the mind. They build self-esteem through their mindful movement activities.

When students Rainbow Play they use mindful movement postures as tools for expression in creative movement stories. This mind/body exercise, allows students to become aware of the physical and mental connection within them. Their new awareness enables them to be present in the moment, which promotes greater objectivity about situational outcomes. The by-product of this experience is one of inner peace and increased self-confidence. The following lesson may be used to instruct students how to form their body for various movement exercises.

ANTICIPATORY SET
FOCUS - To learn mindful movement.
PURPOSE - To associate the posture with its name.
To assume postures safely for use in movement stories.
To learn body awareness.
MOTIVATION - Show a picture depicting the visual image suggested for each posture. Discuss the subject in the picture. Discuss the characteristics of the image. For Example a Flamingo may be described as graceful and steady. A Volcano may be described as active and volatile.
TRANSFER - Explain to the students that when in a posture, it is helpful to visualize the image in their mind. The student imagines the subject while in that particular posture.

OBJECTIVE
The student will focus his attention to imitate the postures and use his imagination while following the teachers' lead.
The student will recognize a posture by its name and know how to position his body to get into posture.
The student will be able to recall the posture for use in movement stories.

INPUT & MODELING
1. Motivational activity.
2. Teacher shows illustration of Posture. (Reproduce for use on an overhead projector)
3. The teacher will explain how students enter into position, one movement at a time.
4. Teacher repeats each movement and moves her body slowly into position as she explains.
5. As teacher leads the movement, students try the posture.

CHECKING FOR UNDERSTANDING
6. Teacher asks if there are any questions.
7. Teacher makes sure all children have a chance to ask questions.

GUIDED PRACTICE
8. Teacher has several students move into the posture while she monitors their work. Other students must watch for reinforcement. Teacher corrects any incorrect movements and has any student who makes a mistake repeat the movement. Teacher continues until all students know the posture.

CLOSURE
9. Teacher reviews posture a couple times that day. Teacher reviews posture at least 1x a day for a week. The last day of review, teacher may ask students how they feel when they release the posture. Students learn 1 posture a day. Each day as they learn new postures they will practice the postures from the previous day and add on the new posture until all postures have been mastered. When students know 10 postures they may begin using postures for movement stories.
10. Continue teaching postures daily. As students learn new postures, their stories will become more involved.
11. The emotional feeling attached to each posture is key to creating stories. Be sure to practice connecting feelings to postures before attempting to have children create stories.

INDEPENDENT PRACTICE
A classroom center devoted to stress management is a good place for practice. Students may practice all quiet Rainbow Play techniques in the center. Explain to students how these exercises may be practiced out side school. You may suggest using mindful movement exercises as a positive way to begin the day. Practicing postures will help them think more clearly.

EXTENSION
The postures in this book are a basis for getting started. Check the materials section in the back of the book for references to expand your knowledge of exercises. Two useful postures that are not illustrated in this book are Lightening Bolt and Crocodile.

MINDFUL MOVEMENT POSTURES

A full description and illustrated outline for postures on the following pages may be reproduced for use on an overhead projector. Use the following guidelines when engaging in exercises.

Suggested Guidelines for Practicing Mindful Movement:
1. Wait at least an hour after eating a full meal.
2. Best if done in bare feet or flat rubber soled shoes.
3. Move slowly and concentrate.
4. If something hurts, don't do it!

When introducing each new pose, you may wish to show a picture as a stimulus for visual imagery. It may be easier for children to remember a posture by its image. For example, the image for Basic Prone is a horse. Use the name "Horse" pose. See page 104 for sample routines.

Standing Poses – The basic stance for all standing positions is Mountain Pose.

Mountain Pose

Stand tall and solid like a mountain.
Your feet are together, arms at your side, shoulders are relaxed, rolled back and down.
Stay balanced by keeping your toes and the heels of your feet planted firmly on the ground.
Imagine your head is the top of the mountain reaching toward the sky,
close your eyes and breath deeply.

Visual Image – A strong, solid mountain.
Affirmation – I am strong, proud, and beautiful like a tall mountain.

Volcano Pose

Begin in Mountain Pose. Relax your shoulders. Jump your feet wide apart.
Bring your hands together in prayer position at your heart. Stretch your hands up to the sky.
Keep eyes focused on hands. Imagine you are an erupting volcano.
Open your arms out to the side and back to your heart. Repeat several times.

Visual Image - An erupting volcano.
Affirmation - I am powerful and lively like an active Volcano.

Tree Pose

Begin in Mountain Pose. When you are ready, press your left foot into the ground and raise your right foot off the ground. Place the sole of your right foot against the inner leg by your knee or higher if possible. Look at an object in front of you to help you balance. Keep your left leg straight and rooted like a tree trunk and your right knee should be pressed out and open. Bring your arms out to the side or above your head with palms together facing each other. Focus on the spot in front of you and breathe deeply. Repeat on other side. Imagine your feet are the roots of the tree growing deep into the ground and your arms are branches growing high toward the sky.

Visual Image - A beautiful leafy tree.
Affirmation - I am hardy and vibrant like a towering tree.

Standing Cobra Pose

Stand in Mountain pose. Stretch your arms behind you and clasp your hands.
Straighten your arms and lift upward. Arch your back slightly and look up.
Remember to breathe. Raise arms as you lift your chest. Tuck your tailbone under.
When you are ready, release your hands. Drop your arms down to your sides.

Visual Image - A snake raising his head toward the sky, his lower body balancing him still on the ground.
Affirmation - I am keen and limber like a wiry snake.

Standing Cat Pose

Stand in Mountain pose. Bring your arms in front of you and clasp your hands.
Keep your hands clasped, turn your arms inside out, (knuckles facing your body)
round your back and look down at your chest. Remember to breathe.
When you are ready, release your arms down to your sides.

Visual Image - A cat standing on its hind legs, curling its spine and stretching its upper paws outward (Scary Halloween cat).
Affirmation - I am clever and agile (active) like a playful cat.

Half Moon Pose

Stand in Mountain pose. Raise your arms over your head. Place the palms of your hands together and fold your thumbs over each other. Press your left foot into the ground and bend your body to the side. Imagine your belly button is sinking into your spine. When you are ready, release. Repeat on the other side.

Visual Image - A white - gold, glowing, half moon, high in the sky.
Affirmation - I am cool and calm like the magnificent moon.

Triangle Pose

Begin in Mountain Pose. Jump your feet wide apart. Raise your arms out to the side, palms facing down. Turn your right foot out, so your toes and your fingers are facing the same direction. Your right heel is facing the arch of your left foot. Push your left hip toward your left hand and bend your upper body to the right. Place your right hand on your right ankle. Roll your tummy up. Look up toward your left thumb. Remember to breathe. Come out of the pose by turning your head toward your right leg. Bend your knee and come up. Place your feet forward and relax your arms down to the side. Repeat on the other side. Return to Mountain Pose.

Visual Image - A bright yellow, triangle shape.
Affirmation - I am brave and daring like a fixed triangle.

Warrior Pose

Begin in Mountain Pose. Jump your feet wide apart.
Raise your arms out to the side, palms facing down.
Turn your right foot out, so your toes and your fingers are facing the same direction.
Your right heel is facing the arch of your left foot.
Bend your right knee. Relax.
Turn your head toward the fingertips of your right hand. Release. Repeat on opposite side.

Visual Image - A strong soldier.
Affirmation - I am intense and courageous like a spirited soldier.

Flamingo Pose

Begin in Mountain Pose. Place an object about 12 inches in front of you.
Use the object to help you focus your attention. Breathe in and out.
Press one leg into the ground and raise the other leg behind you.
Open your arms out to the sides of your body like the wings of a flamingo.
Balance. Repeat on the other leg.

Visual Image - A beautiful pink flamingo.
Affirmation - I am graceful and steady like a lovely Flamingo.

Hands/Knees Poses - The basic position for all Hands/knees positions is Basic Prone (Horse).

Horse Pose

Kneel on all fours. Place your hands underneath your shoulders and knees under your hips.
Your back and neck are straight and your eyes are looking at the floor.

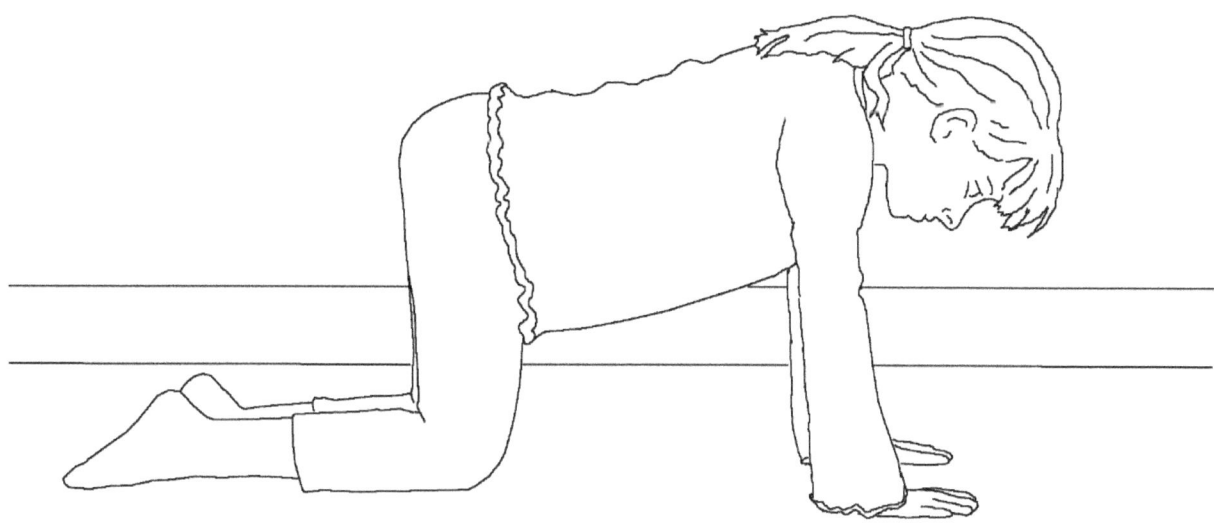

Visual Image - A horse.
Affirmation - I am sturdy and vibrant like a healthy horse.

Cat Pose

Begin on your hands and knees. Arms under your shoulders, palms flat and fingers spread apart.
Your knees are under your hips and toes point back.
Round your spine, look toward your chest and draw your belly button in toward your back.
Remember to breathe. When you are ready, release and flatten your back.

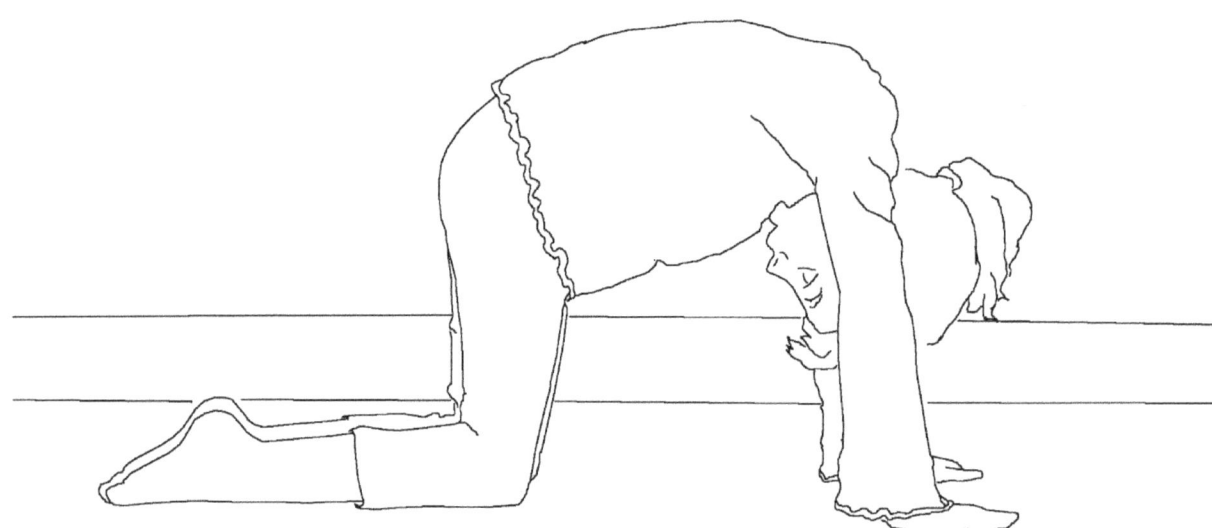

Visual Image - A tabby cat arching his back to stretch.
Affirmation - I am skilled and energetic like a sleek cat.

Child's Pose

Begin on your hands and knees. Draw your bottom back toward the heels of your feet and rest your arms around to your sides with palms facing upward. Let your shoulders drop toward the floor, relax, and breathe.
Use this pose to rest in between postures.

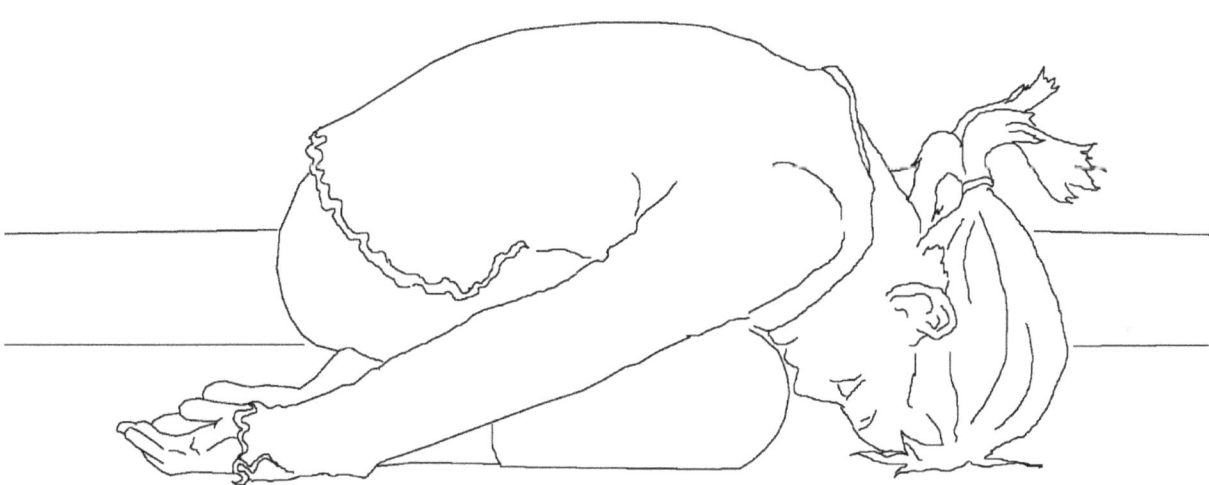

Visual Image - An infant resting in his crib.
Affirmation - I am peaceful and still like a sleeping baby.

Cow Pose

Begin on your hands and knees. Draw your belly button toward your back.
Arch your back. At the same time, lift your head and bottom toward the sky, and look up.
Breathe. When you are ready, release and flatten your back.

Visual Image - A spotted cow in a pasture looking up at the sky.
Affirmation - I am at ease in my body like a comfortable cow.

Dog Pose

Begin on your hands and knees.   Straighten your knees. Point your bottom upward
and press your chest toward your thighs.
Straighten your knees and arms so your body is like a V shape.
Flatten the soles of your feet on the ground. Let your head relax. Remember to breathe.
When you are ready, come back down on your hands and knees. Relax.

Visual Image - A beautiful dog (describe a kind of dog) stretching after taking a nap.
Affirmation - I am constant and vigilant like a loyal dog.

Frog Pose

Begin on your hands and knees. Slide knees and feet wide apart and turn feet outward.
Bring your arms to the ground and clasp your hands together.
Bend your elbows so they form a triangle. Place your weight on your forearms for support.
Press through your bottom downward.
Press through the top of your head. Imagine your spine lengthening.
Slowly lift and lower your tailbone.

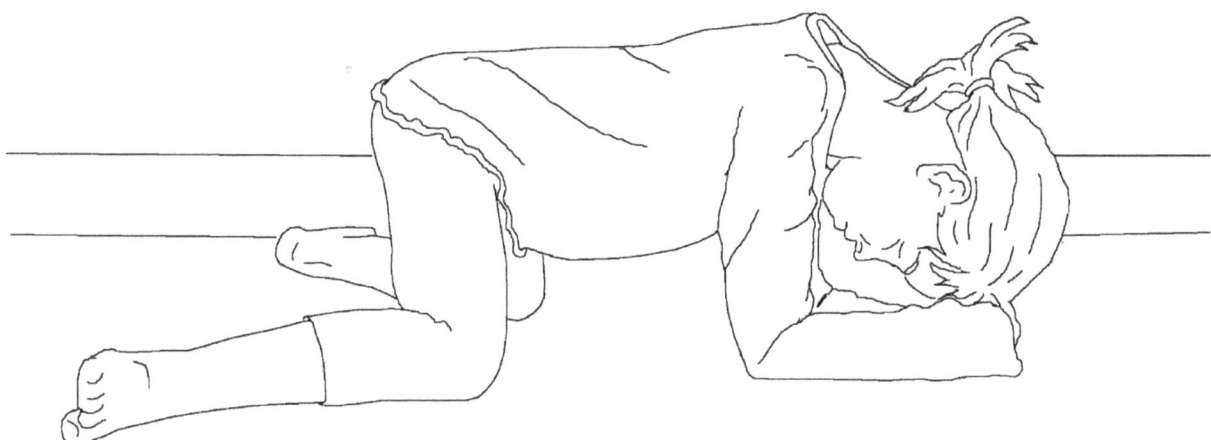

Visual Image - An emerald green frog sitting on a lily pad.
Affirmation - I am poised and alert like an active frog.

Cobra Pose

Lie down on your belly. Your hands are below your shoulders and your elbows are close to your sides. As you lift your chest off the ground, straighten your arms and raise your chin. Stretch your neck and look up toward the sky. Pressing below your hips into the ground. Remember to breathe. When you are ready, slowly roll your chest back down to the ground and bend your elbows so your forearms are resting on the ground.

Visual Image - A slithery cobra raising its head high above the tall grass.
Affirmation - I am clever and slick like a slinky snake.

Pigeon Pose

Begin on your hands and knees. Sit back on your heels.
Slide your left knee forward in front of your hip and bring your shin to the ground.
Angle your foot in front of your right hip and point your toes.
Straighten your right leg back, toes pointed, knee slightly bent.
Move your hands back toward your hips, lift your chest and slightly arch your back.
Lift through the crown of your head. Relax and breathe.

Visual Image - A pigeon sitting on a tall building taking a look at the scenery.
Affirmation - I am confident like a resourceful pigeon.

Lion Pose

Begin on your hands and knees. Sit back on your heels and rest your hands on your knees.
Widen your eyes and stick out your tongue as you move the trunk of your body forward.
Spread your fingers apart. You should feel a stretch in all the muscles of your face and neck.
Imagine you are a ferocious lion. Roar like a lion, if you feel the urge.
Slowly place your tongue back in your mouth. Relax your eyes and fingers.
Sit back on your heels and rest. Repeat.

Visual Image - A ferocious lion.
Affirmation - I am courageous and skillful like a powerful lion.

Seated Poses - The basic position for all seated poses is Easy Seated Pose (Bell).

Bell Pose

Sit on the ground and cross your legs at the ankle or shins, feet away from your bottom.
Keep your back straight, your shoulders relaxed and down away from your ears.
Head is lifted, look straight ahead, and relax your hands on your thighs.
Focus on your breath for a couple minutes. Repeat with the other leg crossed in front.

Visual Image - A shiny silver bell.
Affirmation - I'm bright and beautiful like a sparkling bell.

Butterfly Pose

Begin in Easy Seated Pose. Bring the soles of your feet together.
Allow your knees to sink into the ground. Move your knees slowly like the wings of a butterfly.
Keep your head lifted. You may use your fingers as antennae at the top of your head.

Visual Image - A colorful butterfly.
Affirmation - I'm free and easy like a delicate butterfly.

Diamond Pose

Begin in Easy Seated Pose. Bring the soles of your feet together.
Allow your knees to sink into the ground. Your back is straight. Grasp your feet with your hands.
Round your spine and bend forward. Try to touch your forehead to your feet.
Relax and breathe.

Visual Image - A sparkling diamond.
Affirmation - I'm brilliant and spectacular like a stunning diamond.

Fan or "Peanut Butter and Jelly" Pose

Begin in Easy Seated Pose. Outstretch legs in front of you.
Flex your feet, lift your chest and relax your shoulders back and down.
Imagine yourself a string puppet with a string attached to your spine.
Your spine lengthens as the attached string is pulled above you.
Lift through the crown of your head.
Bend forward from your hips and try to rest your chest on your thighs,
and allow the forehead to rest on your shins.
Hold and breathe. Release and relax.

Visual Image - A hand held fan being closed.
Affirmation - I am unique and special like an ornamental fan.

Lying Down Poses - The basic position for all lying poses is Relaxation Pose (Sleeping Beauty).

Sleeping Beauty Pose (Handsome Prince)

Lie on your back, legs bent with feet hip distance apart.
Your arms by your side and your hands are face up. Relax and breathe.

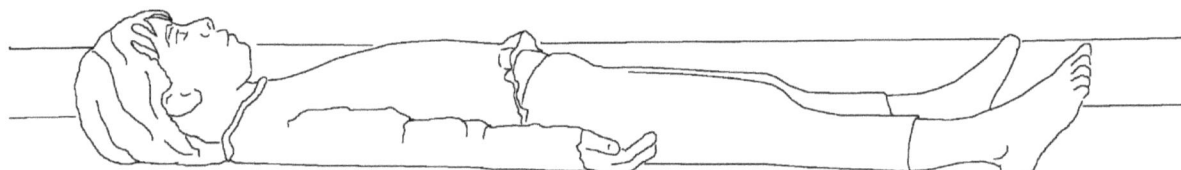

Visual Image - Sleeping Beauty
Affirmation - I am peaceful and serene like sleeping beauty.

Crab Pose

Begin in Relaxation Pose. Bend your knees and place the soles of your feet flat on the ground. Tuck your tailbone and slowly lift your lower spine off the floor one vertebra at a time until you get to your shoulders. Once the hips are up, bend your elbows and hold your waist. Hold this position and breathe. Slowly lower the spine one vertebra at a time.

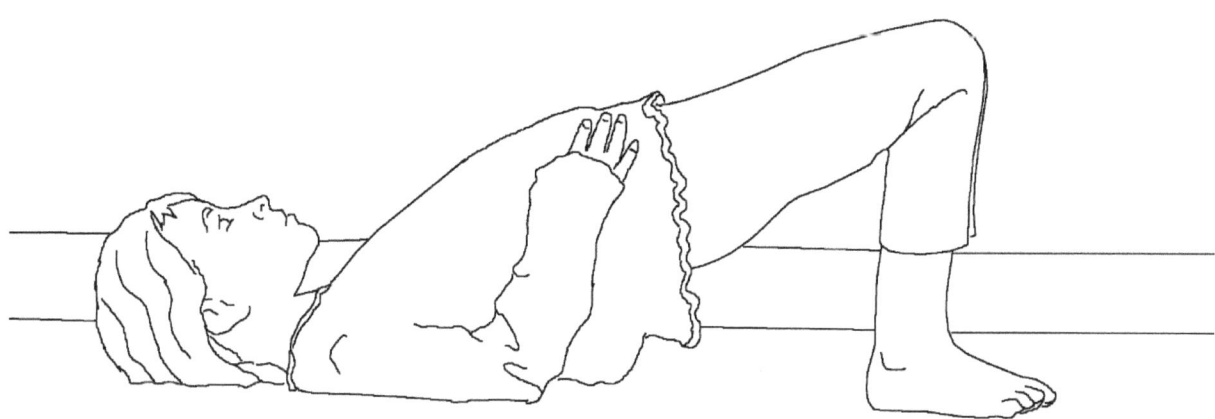

Visual Image - A sea crab.
Affirmation - I am swift like a feisty sea crab.

Potato Bug Pose

Begin in Relaxation Pose. Bring each knee to your chest one at a time.
Hug your knees, bringing your knees close to your body. Hold and breathe.
Place the palms of your hands on your knees. Straighten your elbows as you gently
push your knees away from you. Curl your tailbone up and bring the knees toward your chest.
Practice Potato Bug by bringing your knees away from your chest and toward your chest several times.

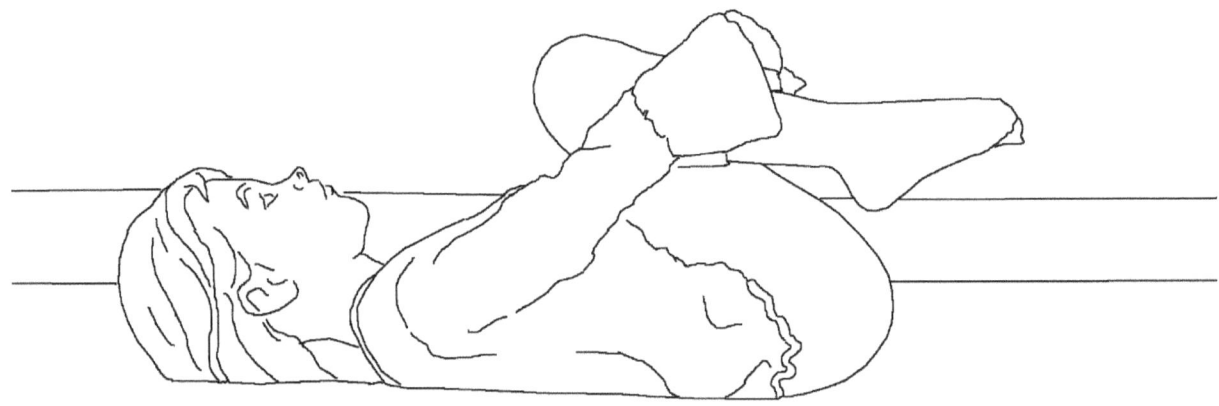

Visual Image - A frightened potato bug.
Affirmation - I am flexible and responsive like a comfortable potato bug.

Candle Pose

Begin in Relaxation Pose. Bend your knees. Swing your legs up overhead.
Place your hands on your lower back and hips for support.

Visual Image - A candle burning brightly.
Affirmation - I am a glowing light like a shimmering candle.

Chapter 3

PAY ATTENTION!

FOCUSED AWARENESS

Focused Awareness exercises teach the student to observe his mind at work. Students can learn to gently pull their minds back to their focus without fighting with themselves. That is, when stray thoughts enter they can observe them, discard them easily, and return back to their task at hand without turmoil and struggle. Practicing focused awareness exercises on a daily basis enhances ones ability to concentrate and relax. Students learn how to spend more time in the present moment rather then waste their energy worrying about past and future events. The result is a student who values the quality of his life experience.

Almost anything we do can become a focused awareness exercise as long as we are conscious of where we choose to focus our attention. When we focus our mind on what we are doing from moment to moment we become aware. Being aware of what you are doing while you are doing it is the heart of conscious living. Focused Awareness exercises practiced regularly may have a powerful effect on a student's reality. It can change the way a student perceives life. When one is conscious one values themselves and others more. The following exercise may be used to instruct students on the concept of focused awareness exercises.

ANTICIPATORY SET
FOCUS - Focused Awareness
PURPOSE - To strengthen concentration and learn how to relax.
MOTIVATION - Ask students to talk about their favorite toy or activity. Open a discussion about how involved they become and how they feel while participating in the activity or playing with the toy.
TRANSFER - Explain how they are going to learn how to give the same kind of attention to everything they do. The way they will learn is by practicing how to focus on different objects and experiences.

OBJECTIVE
The student will observe the body and mind while focusing on an experience.

INPUT & MODELING
1. Motivational Activity.
2. Explain that eating is an experience. Discuss how we sometimes gobble food without even noticing how it tastes or anything else about it. During this exercise students are going to observe their body and their mind while eating pretzels (Cheerios, raisins, peanuts, etc.).
3. Teacher will explain that she is going to guide them through the exercise and they must think about each question she asks while very slowly eating the pretzel.
4. Teacher will model exercise for students before guiding them through their own practice (Record a modified version of the exercise on audio tape for use while modeling).
5. Teacher plays recording and begins exercise as students observe.

CHECK FOR UNDERSTANDING
6. Teacher asks students what they noticed about her exercise. She may want to ask more specific questions. Example, "Did I eat quickly or slowly?"
7. Teacher asks students if they have any questions.

GUIDED PRACTICE

8. Explain that everybody will be given 1 to 3 pretzels but they are not to touch them until they are told to touch them.

9. Hand out pretzels. Explain that they will eat the pretzels one at a time as you ask questions and instruct them to eat the next one.

10. Teach that almost anything we do may become a focused awareness exercise as long as we are conscious of where we choose to focus our attention. When we focus our mind on what we are doing each moment we become aware. Being aware of what we do while we do it is the core of these exercises.

11. Instruct them to observe the pretzel as if they had never seen a pretzel and to look at it from a baby's perspective. Ask, " What color is it? What shape? How does it feel in your hands, between your fingers? What is the texture? Smooth? Bumpy? Smell it. How does it smell? Do any thoughts come to your mind? Do you have any thoughts or feelings about the pretzel? Does it bring up any memories? Finally, have them focus their attention on eating the pretzel. Tell them to experience every action involved. Have them notice how they move their arm, bending at the elbow and bringing the pretzel to their lips with their hand. Have them notice how they place it in their mouth, how it feels on their tongue, on their teeth, and how it tastes. Tell them to chew it slowly and completely. When they are ready to swallow, have them pay attention to how it feels as it moves down their throat. How do they feel once the pretzel has been eaten? Repeat with other two pretzels.

CLOSURE

12. Ask students what it felt like to observe their physical sensations and thoughts while eating the pretzels. Discuss it.

13. If students are old enough they might journal about the experience or teacher may choose to do a class journal with younger students.

INDEPENDENT PRACTICE

A classroom center devoted to stress management is a good place for practice. Students may practice all quiet Rainbow Play techniques in the center.

See Reproducibles for worksheet. You may administer worksheet orally to younger students. After using various Focused Awareness exercises with students, begin giving them opportunities to integrate the exercises into their life outside of school. For example, explain they might go to an empty room when there is chaos in the house and try an exercise they have already practiced with you.

EXTENSION

Practice focused awareness exercises daily to enhance student's ability to concentrate and relax. Use aromatherapy and music to effect a mood change. See Chapter 6 for resources.

FOCUSED AWARENESS ACTIVITIES

Activity A
Choose a CD with music that expresses various mood changes (See Suggested Materials). Separate children into groups of equal number. Children are assigned numbers within each group. Spaces have been designated at start of game. For example in the left corner of the room is the barn, in the right corner is the stable, in the far left is the zoo and the far right is the jungle. Explain to children that they will think of a mindful movement posture that matches how they feel when they hear the music. When the music begins the instructor will call for all the number 1's to move into a separate space. Children will move to their space and freeze in the posture they have chosen when the music stops.
Teacher will continue calling assigned numbers; students may dance to music in yoga character. Each child within a group will become a statue each time the music stops.
This sequence will continue until everyone in the groups has been called and statues have been formed. When the final song plays, students will dance in character.

Activity B
Choose a CD with music that expresses various mood changes.
Match actions such as marching, tippy-toes, giant steps, skipping, hopping, running, and walking with the different musical pieces.
Have children learn which actions go with each musical piece.
Once this process is complete - play the musical pieces periodically and have children match the actions on their own.
Variation: Try playing an instrumental piece and as you fade the music have students move into a mindful movement posture that feels natural with the action already taking place.
Variation: Use a drum to create various beats. Have children march, tippy toe, and take giant steps, skip, hop, run and walk to the different beats of the drum.
Variation: This may also be done with beanbags. Have students sit in a circle. Use actions such as balancing on the head, shaking, tossing, hand-to-hand, etc.
This can be done in a stop/start fashion or if a remote is available skip around the CD. Children will need to listen for the change in tempo.

Activity C
Sing a verse. Teach children the verse. For example sing Twinkle, Twinkle Little Star and place clapping or a rattle sound in-between words or verses. Tell children you are going to periodically place a different sound or verse in between the main verse and they have to keep track of the number of times the different sound or verse is inserted. They will keep track with a show of fingers.

Activity D
Echo - This is a version of following the leader without a lot of movement. Children sit in a circle. They are to watch you for action and after every new action they must echo you. Examples of actions may be a sound, singing, clapping, stomping, mouth clicking, face slapping etc.

Activity E
Animal Partner Sounds - Children are paired and given an animal sound to remember. For example, You have 5 groups of 2, Pair 1 makes the cow sound "moo", Pair 2 makes the cat sound "meow", Pair 3 makes the dog sound "woof", Pair 4 makes the frog sound "rib bit" and Pair 5 makes the pigeon sound "coo coo". All children sit against the wall. Two pairs go at one time. One child from each pair is placed somewhere in the room. The other child from each pair is blindfolded. The children placed within the room repeat their sound over and over again until the blindfolded partner finds them. When the pairs are matched they sit down and watch until all children have had a chance. At the end all children come together in their poses, cow, frog, cat, dog and pigeon and create sound and movement for their animal. It is noisy but fun!!!

Activity F
Sniffing Detectives – Choose a variety of oils about six and place a drop or two on cotton balls. Keep the same scented balls in the same group. Place balls in small containers, for example film canisters. Randomly pass out containers to students. Instruct students to open containers and sniff the enclosed cotton. Then students are to mingle with one another and find students with the same scented cotton ball as their own. Eventually small groups of students will form with the same scent.

Activity G
Have children assume a posture. Then have the children move in that posture. For Example, all children in dog pose walk slowly, walk quickly. Use a drum to pace their movement. When you stop drumming children freeze. You tell them to assume the new posture.

Activity H
Sensory Awareness

Sense - Object

Tasting - Pretzel	Seeing - Blade of Grass
Touching - Cotton	Smelling - Chocolate
Hearing - Music	

Above are examples of objects to use in this exercise. Have students' focus their thoughts on the actual object for 4 days, on the 5th day have them use their imagination to focus on the same object. They may pretend they have the actual object. As with the example of the pretzel, students go through all the same motions as when they actually had the pretzel in front of them.

Pre-school Variation: Have students focus their thoughts on the actual object. Have student's tell you about the object. The color, shape, size, smell, how it feels, etc. Have them try to draw the object. You can also take the object away and have them try to draw from memory.

Other: Ask children how the particular object makes them feel. Then give children magazines and have them cut out pictures that make them feel the same way as the object makes them feel. For example, if the object is cheese and it makes them feel comfortable, what can they find in the magazine that makes them feel comfortable? Cut the pictures out and put them together in a collage. This can also be done with postures or after a journey. Talk about the feelings and then follow up with a collage.

EMOTIONS
Have students remember an emotion, such as anger, and the details of how it felt when they experienced the emotion in a particular situation. Ask them to think about what "angered" them. What physical sensations did they feel? What thoughts were they having at the time they became angry? Ask them to remember where they were, whom they were with, what they did, etc. After the exercise is complete, have students write in their journals. Have students focus on a different emotion each day. At the end of the week, students use each day's emotions to assemble postures for use in a movement story.
Variation - Teacher may choose to use written journals as a form of feedback. For example - Student writes, "I was so angry, I hit Johnny". Teacher writes, "How might the situation have been different if you chose to walk away?" "Or if Johnny walked away? Students respond in writing to teacher feedback.
Variation - Teacher may choose to have students create a piece of artwork to express their emotions.

List of Adjectives:
Aggressive, agonized, anxious, apologetic, bashful, blissful, bored, cautious, confident, determined, disappointed, disgusted, ecstatic, enraged, envious, exasperated, exhausted, frightened, frustrated, guilty, happy, horrified, hurt, idiotic, jealous, lonely, mischievous, miserable, optimistic, perplexed, puzzled, regretful, relieved, sad, joyful, satisfied, thoughtful.

List of Nouns:
Love, forgiveness, trustworthiness, loyalty, compassion, hatred, honesty, spontaneity, ambition, consideration, respect, freedom, appreciation, adventure, betrayal, abandonment, confrontation, expectation, conflict, comfort, possessiveness, acceptance.

ADVANCED
Breathing - Focus on counting the breath, breathe in on the count of five, breathe out on the count of five (length of practice will vary according to age and experience).
Variation: Focus on breathing without counting. Being with each breath and pay attention to the rise and fall of the belly. If your mind wonders, bring it back to the breath.

Sound - Listen to a piece of instrumental music. Listen to each note and the spaces between; imagine the music moving in and out of your body as you breathe.
Variation: Use sounds rather than music, i.e. the sound of a fan.
Variation: Use of a particular sound, phrase, or affirmation as a point of focus. Repeat the sound over and over again, leave space in between, and continue for a specified length of time. Examples - "I am relaxed". "I am calm".

Walking - Observe how you walk. Pay attention to each step. Notice how your foot feels as it touches the ground, how your feet move, etc.... This may be done outdoors on a nice day.

Visualize - Imagine a natural object. For example, imagine the waves of the ocean or focus on organs of the body or a color.

Gazing - Focus on an object with your eyes open. A piece of grass, a picture, a candle, or the tip of your nose, etc.

Pre-school Variation:
THOUGHTFUL PLAY EXERCISES

It may be useful to play soft music in the background while children participate in some of these activities. Other activities call for lively music. See suggestions for CD's in back of book.

1. Picking Flowers (Fake Garden) or Collecting Flowers - place in a basket. Studying Flowers (dissecting and grouping the parts leaves, stems, petals.) Using in an art project.
2. Picking Berries - putting in bucket (CLASS FIELD TRIP)
3. Nature Walks - Give different groups different collectable - collecting sticks, stones, leaves, acorns, etc. Then have children create collages with what they collected.
4. Scooping or raking dried beans, rice, sand, etc., placing in container.
5. Watching ant farms, fish tanks, etc. Talking about what they observed and creating artwork afterwards.
6. Simple Tasks - Cutting simple shapes or paper strips, drawing lines, filling and dumping containers of water, counting collectibles and putting items in box, stringing beads, sewing, making chain links, marble painting in a box, paper maze, building with popsicle sticks, etc. Several activities could be done at one time in groups, have groups rotate stations.
7. Separating objects into categories - color, shape, size, etc.
8. Matching textures, letters, shapes, colors.
9. Tracing patterns.

Advanced Pre-school

10. Breathing - Focus on counting the breath. Teacher counts as children breathe in on the count of three and breathe out on the count of three. This is very brief at the pre-school level. Variation: Focus on breathing without counting. Being with each breath and pay attention to the rise and fall of the belly. Placing a beanbag on the child's belly will help focus their attention. If your mind wonders, bring it back to the beanbag.

11. Sound - Listen to a short piece of instrumental music. Imagine the music-moving coming in through your head and out through your toes.
Variation: Use an instrument. Example drums sticks. Children echo the sounds you make with your instrument, with their instrument.

12. Gazing - Focus on an object with your eyes open. A piece of grass, a picture, a candle, or the tip of your nose, etc. Have children discuss the properties of these objects with you. Write in a class journal and draw a picture for the class. After studying an object have children draw a picture of the object themselves.

13. Toss the beanbag back and forth from hand to hand. Balancing the beanbag on your head and walking. Balancing the beanbag on your feet in candle pose. Balancing the beanbag with a body part and figuring out how to move the body to make it work, walk, crawl, etc. To enhance social skills and problem solving together, they balance the beanbags with a friend -- no hands, and each partner has to be touching the bag. Tossing the beanbag back and forth with a partner. Toss beanbag till the music stops.

CHAPTER 4

IMAGINE!

IMAGINARY JOURNEY WORK

Imaginary Journey Work is a technique, which uses the imagination to promote relaxation. The teacher, in a calm voice, guides the students through an imaginary journey of the mind by describing a relaxing experience. Students listen, breathe deeply, and visualize the scenario in their mind. This technique allows students to let go of stressful thoughts. Students are able to calm their mind and heart. It is also an excellent tool used as a stimulus for writing in journals. Imaginary Journey Work may also be used to focus the mind when it is scattered. It may be used at various points through out the day when students need a little extra help staying on task. After children complete an imaginary journey exercise, discuss how they feel out loud (write a class journal if students are young). If students are older, have them think about how they felt and write their feelings in their journals. Students may choose to share their feelings in a group discussion, through a creative movement exercise, by creating a piece of artwork or not at all depending on the particular objective.

At the preschool level this technique may be an active experience, allowing children to go through the motions of the journey. It is also an excellent tool used as a stimulus for drawing. Imaginary Journey Work at the pre-school level gives students an opportunity to explore their imagination, focus their mind and helps to develop attention to staying on task. After children complete an imaginary journey exercise, discuss how they feel out loud. Students may share their feelings in a group discussion, through creative movement, by creating a piece of artwork or not at all depending on the particular objective.

ANTICIPATORY SET
FOCUS - Imaginary Journey Work as a tool for relaxation and balancing the mind and body.
PURPOSE - To focus the mind when it is scattered. To heighten awareness and learn how to value feelings.
MOTIVATION - Use pictures that evoke images of the setting you would like to have students imagine or set up a corner of the room and decorate it to imitate the experience you want them to imagine. You might ask questions to help children recall similar experiences.
TRANSFER - Explain that you will guide them in an imaginary journey within their body.

OBJECTIVE
The student will be able to focus his mind and attain a sense of inner balance by connecting his body and mind through the process of imaginary journeywork.

INPUT & MODELING
1. Motivational activity.
2. Explain that students will assume a position. There are several positions you may choose to use (lying on the floor, standing in mountain pose, standing in tree pose, or sitting on the floor/ in a chair, feet on floor). Eyes will be closed.
3. Show them the position they will use for this exercise.
4. Explain that they will listen to you describe an experience and they are to imagine they are part of that experience. Instruct them to keep their eyes closed and to listen. Talking, touching, opening their eyes will ruin the experience.

CHECK FOR UNDERSTANDING
5. Ask students if they have any questions about what they are supposed to do.
6. Answer all questions.

GUIDED PRACTICE
7. Have students stand in Mountain pose.
8. In a calm voice, begin describing an experience.
9. "Imagine you are a tree, among other tall trees in a huge, beautiful, lush forest. The forest is dark except for a small clearing in the sky where the sun is shining through, allowing a stream of white gold light to illuminate your branches. Focus your energy on your feet; imagine your feet as roots of the tree growing deeply into the ground, deep into the center of the earth. Feel the warmth of the sun penetrate your branches and move through your trunk down through your roots, giving you strength and energy. A light warm rain falls softly upon your branches providing you with moisture to help you grow. Feel your roots drinking in this thirst quenching liquid. See your roots growing deep into the center of the earth. Imagine the earths colors, brown, red and gold mixed together as your roots penetrate the earth deeper and deeper into the center. Notice how you feel. Are you happy? Peaceful, Calm? Relaxed? Energized? Balanced? Now slowly wiggle your toes and fingers. Slowly open your eyes."

CLOSURE
10. Discuss how the experience made the students feel.
11. Write a class journal or have students' journal independently about their feelings.
12. Have students draw an outline of the body on paper. Tell them to think about how they felt during the exercise. Use colors to represent feelings and color in the parts of the body. They can journal afterwards in dialogue form. For example, "Chest" talks with "Michael" about how it feels.

INDEPENDENT PRACTICE
Imaginary Journey tapes may be placed in a center for individual use. Give students suggestions for using imaginary journey's at home. They might try their own imaginary journeys (created using in-school worksheet – see Chapter 7) before going to bed at night or at other times when they need to feel at peace.

EXTENSION
Students may express feelings in a creative movement story. Teacher may also use imaginary journeywork periodically to help children focus their mind and center themselves. Try creating your own imaginary journey exercise. Have students create one of their own. (See Chapter 7)

EXERCISES

The following descriptions are to help you get started. Some are intended for use while being still; others are intended for use as an active journey. Read them over and think about how you might use them. You may choose to extend them and/or play music in the background use your own words keeping with the basic concept. Use Imaginary journeys as a stimulus to write a class poem. When you've written a poem, use it to create a group movement story. Feel free to experiment. Children's Book of Yoga and Fly Like a Butterfly will be especially useful for this section.

Fly Like a Bird (Day Break) Suggested Time- 3:29
Imagine you are a beautiful blue bird. You are perched on a branch, high up in a towering tree. The branches are so tall its as if they reach the sky. You have keen eyesight, sharp hearing and you are very aware of your surroundings. You hear the sounds of nature around you. You smell the sweet warm air. Below you, you see the bright green blades of grass. Under the grass you see the golden brown earth. Crawling in the dark moist soil are bugs and squiggly long worms that you will eat for supper later in the day but you are not hungry now. You feel adventurous. You peer up above and marvel at the beauty of the bright blue sky and the soft white fluffy clouds. You spread your wings and allow the force of the wind to lift you up off the branch. You begin to fly high in the soft blue sky. You feel happy and excited. You soar high up above the white marshmallow clouds. Your body is light as a feather. All your worries drift away as you carry your self higher and higher into the earth's atmosphere. You are peaceful and carefree. The warmth of the yellow sun wraps itself around you like a golden, white blanket. Allow yourself to relax. Breathe and be still (10 seconds). You allow the blanket to gently drop off and you spread your wings once more. You slowly fly down toward the tall tree. You spot your cozy nest and softly land in its comfort. You snuggle up; close your eyes and rest. Your journey was long and now you are at peace in the comfort of your home. Breathe and be still (15 seconds). Curl to one side. Wiggle your fingers and toes. Stretch. Gently push yourself up into bell pose.

Playground (Day Break) Suggested Time- 3:41
Imagine any park with a playground where you have enjoyed yourself. Now see yourself in that park on a beautiful sunny day. Pause 10 seconds. Pick a comfortable spot to sit down and begin to breath deeply. Imagine the suns white, golden light softly flowing over your head, neck, and shoulders. It warms you and relaxes you as it pours over each part of your body. Down your arms (pause-3 seconds), over you're upper and lower body (pause- 3 seconds) and down your legs and feet (pause-3 seconds). You feel a gentle breeze upon your skin. Look around the park, what do you see? There are many rides. Pick your favorite ride. Maybe you like the swings, the slide, the see saw; choose which ever ride you like the most. Now imagine enjoying yourself on this ride (Pause 10 seconds). Listen to the sounds around you. Hear the other children laughing and the birds singing (pause- 3 seconds). At one end of the park there are water sprinklers, listen to the pitter, patter of the water as it splashes the pavement (pause- 3 seconds). Look up at the blue sky and allow yourself to feel peaceful being part of nature. Slowly bring yourself to a still position. Pay attention to how and what you are feeling. Relax and breathe. You are quiet and peaceful at rest with yourself. Pause for 15 seconds. (Suggestion: Remember the feeling of allowing your muscles to relax as each part of your body is covered with warm golden light. You will be able to create that response when you want to relax before a test.) Bring yourself back to your classroom. Listen for me to count from 5 to 1. When I reach 1, slowly wiggle your fingers and toes, and then open your eyes.

Farm (Day Break) Suggested Time- 3:36
Imagine you look outside your window and you are in the country. You see a light blue sky, tall trees, and green grass for miles. It is a crisp autumn day. The sun is shining and the air smells sweet, fresh and clean. The leaves on the trees are beginning to change color. You see gold, orange, and red. It is early morning and you are getting ready to go on a hayride to the apple groves on a farm. You sit on a large rock and wait for the farmer to come in his red wagon to pick you up. The country is quiet and peaceful. Listen to the quiet. (Pause-5 seconds) The farmer drives up, stops, and motions for you to climb into the wagon. You climb in and sit on a bale of hay. All the kids in your class slowly climb onto the wagon too. (Pause-10 seconds) On your journey to the apple grove you pass a vegetable patch. You spy tiny country animals among the greenery. Rabbits, chipmunks, and field mice scurry about getting ready for winter. You feel the breeze against your skin and the movement of the wagon on the dirt road. When you reach the apple grove - you slowly climb out to begin picking apples (5-seconds). There are green apples, yellow apples, and red apples. You choose your favorite color of the three, pick one, and take a bite. The fruit is sweet and juicy. You fill your bag and rest on the hay in the wagon. You are quiet and peaceful (10 seconds). Slowly the wagon moves and the journey back from where you started begins. Enjoy the ride, breathe, and relax. When the wagon stops, I will count back from 5 to 1, when I reach one, slowly wiggle your fingers and toes, and open your eyes.

Beach (Day Break) Suggested Time- 4:30
Imagine you are at a beach, any beach. The beaches of Lake Erie, an ocean beachfront, any beach you choose. Now see yourself on that beach on a beautiful sunny day. (Pause 10 seconds). Pick a comfortable spot to place your towel. Smooth your towel on the sand. Lie down, close your eyes, and begin to breathe deeply. Breathe deep, slow relaxing inhalations and exhalations. (Pause- 5 seconds) Imagine the suns white, golden light softly flowing over your head, neck, and shoulders. This golden, white light falls over your body like a beautiful waterfall of color, releasing all negativity and surrounding you with positive energy. It warms you and relaxes you as it pours over each part of your body. As it flows over your arms (pause- 3 seconds), over you're upper and lower body (pause – 3 seconds) and down your legs and feet (pause - 3 seconds) it gently cleanses all impurities from you. You feel a light, gentle, breeze blowing and tickling your skin (pause 3 seconds). Listen to the swishing sound the waves make as they roll in and out (3 seconds). Your body sinks in the sand. Feel the heat of the golden, white sun in the soft blue sky above you and the warmth of the sand beneath you. It feels as if you are sinking deeper and deeper into the sand. Every inch of your body tingles with each grain of sand that touches your body. Relax and breathe in this glorious cocoon of white light. (Give them a moment to relax. 5 seconds) How do you feel? Compare this feeling to how you felt before we began. (Suggestion: Remember the feeling of allowing your muscles to relax as each part of your body is covered with warms golden light. Your will be able to create that response when you want to relax before a test.) Listen for me to count from 5 to 1(count). When I reach 1 slowly wiggle your toes and fingers and then open your eyes.

Bouncing Ball (Day Break) Suggested Time- 4:25
Imagine you are in a big, beautiful playroom. The floors are colored brightly with red, yellow, and blue squared flooring. The walls are made of glass so the bright yellow sun shines through on everything in the room. There are sliding glass doors that lead outside into a large green grassy field. The doors are open and you can smell the scent of freshly cut grass. It is a warm spring day and a light breeze passes through the room. You feel the air on your skin. You hear the sound of birds chirping and other children outside laughing and playing. In the middle of the floor are large bouncing balls (the kind with a handle so you can sit on them and hold on). There are balls of every color – pink, blue, orange, yellow, green, purple, and red. You walk over and choose one of the balls. You can choose any colored

ball you like (5 seconds). You grab hold of the handle and sit on the ball. The balls of your feet are lightly touching the floor. You begin bouncing on the ball, up and down, up and down all around the room. Now it is time to go on an adventure to any place you choose. Maybe you would like to bounce to a playground or an amusement park. Maybe you just want to bounce to a big field. You decide it is your adventure. You bounce out the sliding glass doors to a place where you will have fun and will be able to forget your worries and relax and enjoy yourself. Bring yourself there now and try to imagine all the different sound, sights, and smells. You may even imagine how the experience feels. Breathe deeply and relax, I will stay quite for a minute while you breathe and relax. (Pause for about 30 seconds) Now climb off your bouncing ball and lie down in comfortable spot. Let your whole body relax. Your head… your neck…your shoulders…your arms, hands and fingers… your upper body …your lower body…your legs, feet and toes. Breathe and relax. (Suggestion: Remember when you use your breathing as a calming tool, you have the ability to alter the energy in your body. If you feel angry because you are sent to a time out, use your breathing to change the angry energy to peaceful energy. Listen as I count back from 5 to 1, when I reach 1 wiggle your fingers and toes and slowly open your eyes.

The following examples are Imaginary Journey descriptions with specific objectives in mind. When each experience is complete, instruct students to gather art supplies. Give them the opportunity to express their feelings through art. Some students may benefit from this mode of expression.

Forgiveness (Dealing with Feelings) Suggested Time- 5:00
Think of one person you have been angry with and have had a hard time forgiving recently (pause-5 seconds). Keep that person in the back of your mind because we will remember the person later in our journey. Now, as you sit in your chair with your eyes closed, imagine that outside the window you see a large boardwalk, a body of water and a large boat secured on the dock. Slowly, walk out of this room onto that boardwalk over to the boat. Step onto the boat, look around, and smell the fresh air (3 seconds). Now, open the door that leads to the cabin inside the boat. Climb down the stairs into the cabin, and find a seat by a porthole (window -3 seconds). Imagine breathing fresh air in through the pores of your body allowing yourself to relax. Pay attention to the place in your body where you feel the most tension (3 seconds). As you breathe out, allow yourself to relax even more. See the pores in your skin, where the tension lies, as windows opening to let out the anger you feel. Breathe slowly and deeply and relax (3 seconds). Now imagine you are peering through a porthole, a circular window. . Through the window you see the person you are unable to forgive. Allow the entire situation to play back for you like a movie. Remember what occurred that sparked your anger. (Give students' time to really think about the situation -15 seconds). Breathe deeply (10 seconds). As you breathe in imagine healing white light being absorbed into your pores. As you exhale, breathe out anger and resentment. Now imagine the same situation but this time the outcome is different. Think about what would have made the outcome better for you? (15 seconds) Do you have different feelings now? What picture do you imagine that symbolizes how you feel now that the outcome is different? Give students time to think. (Suggestion: Remember you have the ability to control how you respond to your feelings. The next time you are angry remember how you controlled your behavior to change the outcome of the situation.) Listen to my voice count back from 5 to 1. Count. When I reach 1, slowly wiggle your toes and fingers and when you are ready, open your eyes. (Draw or create an artistic piece that embodies the image of forgiveness in your mind.)

Healing with Color (Dealing with Feelings) Suggested Time- 4:56
Close your eyes and begin to breathe slowly and deeply in and out of your nose (3 – seconds). Imagine you walk out of this room and outside there is an elevator. You push the up button and the elevator doors open. You step inside the elevator and push the 5th floor button. Continue breathing slowly and watch each floor button light up as the elevator carries you higher. One… two… three… four… five… before the doors open, imagine a place where you safe, comfortable and relaxed. This place is special to you. It could be a garden, the ocean, or a special room in your house. Any place, you decide, it is your special place. Now see the door open. You step out into your special place (pause-3 seconds). No matter where you are imagine you see a beautiful rainbow either outside a window or up above in the blue sky. Focus on a color of the Rainbow that brings you peace (Pause- 3 seconds). Now, choose an object from this special place. Any object that attracts you, a flower, a cloud, or even a light bulb. Whatever object draws you. Imagine that object filling with your chosen color. Now, imagine your chosen object floating above you. It gently and slowly releases a vapor spraying your body with this colorful mist. Breathe the color in; allow it to penetrate your body through the pores of your skin. It vibrates deep into the center of your being. See the color running through your veins. Allow it to cleanse all impurities from your body. It helps you heal any insecurity you may feel. Now breathe the color out through the pores of your skin and imagine the toxins leaving your body. When all the color has escaped, allow the pores of your skin to close. Be still (5 seconds). Breathe deeply. How do you feel? (10 seconds) (Suggestion: Remember the feeling of safety and how you created healing energy in your body that allowed you to enter this safe place. You will be able to create a safe place for yourself whenever you feel lonely, uncomfortable, or nervous.)
Now slowly walk back to the elevator and push the down button, the doors open, you step inside, push the 1st floor button. Listen to me count down from 5 to 1. As I count, see each button light up; listen to the sounds on the elevator as the elevator carries you down to the 1st floor. Five, four, three, two, one. Now slowly wiggle your toes and fingers. Open your eyes. (Draw or create an artistic piece that expresses how you feel.)

Creativity (Dealing with Feelings) Suggested Time- 2:36
Sit down. Close your eyes. Take three cleansing breaths. Imagine a white and gold light formed like a waterfall flowing through and over your body. As it passes through and over your body, it washes and unblocks any negativity you may be experiencing in the moment. The negativity drains out of you and disappears. Now, imagine you are a container. What do you look like? Do you have a lid? Are you full of any substance? What color are you? What size? What shape? (Pause – 15 seconds) Now see the container you have become. If you don't like the container you have imagined, feel free to change your container. Now what do you see? Is it the same or different? Open your eyes. (Draw the container you imagined.)
These journeys are meant to help children become still and completely relaxed.

Beach (Slumber) Suggested Time- 4:17
Listen to the description of a warm sunny day on the beach and use your imagination to pretend you are experiencing the journey. (grounding).
"We are going on an imaginary journey to the beach. We will take a ship with other children to get there. The captain of the ship says, "all aboard!" You get on the ship with the other children and take a seat on the boat. This trip to the beach will be great to relax and play. We can sit on the shore and look out at the water." Now look out over the water and see the beach in a distance. Feel the wind in your hair and the warmth of the sun of your skin! Feel the boat rock and the water splash on your body. (Pause – 3 seconds) "We are here, lets get out of the boat and walk to the beach. Find a place in the sand to put your towel down." "Now lie out your towel and smooth it out. " Sit back, with your legs

straight out in front, put your toes in the sand, "ooh it feels warm and tingly." Ok, lay down on your back. Now relax and breathe in and out, slowly (pause 3 seconds). Look up in the sky, what do you see? Beautiful white fluffy clouds? A golden, yellow sparkling sun? How does the sun feel? Warm and soothing? Now, see the sun become liquid and slowly pour down from the sky like a waterfall washing over your body. It feels warm and refreshing! Now, look at the clouds and imagine a cloud as a beautiful, white blanket that floats down from the sky and covers you up. Close your eyes, breathe slowly and deeply, and go to sleep. " Music plays about 30 seconds before next journey.

Body of Light (Slumber) Suggested Time- 5:10
Lie down. Close your eyes. Imagine you are lying on the grass in the middle of a field; it is a beautiful spring day. Breathe slowly and deeply (3 –seconds). The sun is a white, golden light. Imagine the white, golden rays of the sun gently pour into your body as you breathe in through your nose. Imagine this light cleansing each part of your body as you breathe it in and imagine breathing out a black mist that carries all your worries and problems away. Now focus your attention on your toes. Breathe in white healing light through your toes (3 seconds). Breathe out a black mist (3 seconds). Imagine the mist carries away all worries and problems. (Lead students through this purification process of the body by slowly focusing on each part of the body until you have covered every section, ending with the crown of the head.) Now imagine breathing the white light through your toes, up through your calves, thighs and into your hips. (3 seconds) Breathe out slowly, a black mist. (3 seconds) Breathe in the white light though your fingertips, up though your arms and into your shoulders. (3 seconds) Slowly breathe out worries and see the black mist disappear into the earth. (3 seconds) Now breathe in the white, golden light through the crown of your heading filling you head, neck, shoulders, upper body, lower body, arms and hands, legs and feet. (10 seconds) Breathe out all worries and fears; release the black mist, out through the crown of your head. (5 seconds) Now imagine your body in a cocoon of white light, floating in space. Relax and breathe. (Pause-10 seconds) Imagine you float slowly back down into the field and are resting. (Pause-10 seconds) Allow yourself to fall asleep.

Clouds (Slumber) Suggested Time- 4:46
Imagine it is a warm sunny day. You walk out of your classroom into a large field. You lie down on a soft, cottony towel in the grassy field. Above you, the sky is blue and full of beautiful white fluffy clouds. Focus on one of the clouds and imagine it turns into a pool of white liquid in a large, light blue pitcher. A tiny fairy tips the pitcher slowly, pouring the liquid over your head and body. As the liquid covers each part of your body, breathe deeply and allow yourself to relax more and more with each exhalation. Relax your head, shoulders, arms, upper body, lower body, legs, and feet. (Pause 15 seconds.) Now see a soft billowy cloud float down, scoop you up, and wrap around you so you feel cozy and warm. It lifts you up into the sky among the other clouds. You feel light as a feather as it carries you higher and higher into the sky above the earth's atmosphere. You are relaxed and calm. The cloud feels like a plush comfortable cushion. The air smells so fresh and clean. Relax and breathe. (Pause 15 seconds) Your ride is ending as the cloud that carries you slowly descends to the earth. It gently lowers you into your seat in your classroom. You feel your feet flat on the floor beneath you. Pay attention to how and what you feel (5 seconds). (Suggestion: Remember the feeling of calm and peace and how you were able to create these feelings whenever you feel nervous or anxious. Listen for me to count from 5 to 1. When I reach 1 slowly wiggle your toes and fingers and then open your eyes.

Variation for the Pre-School Level:
ANTICIPATORY SET
FOCUS - Imaginary Journey Work as a tool for balancing the mind and body.
PURPOSE - To focus the mind when it is scattered. To heighten awareness and learn how to value feelings.
MOTIVATION - Use pictures or actual objects that evoke images of the setting you would like to have students imagine or set up a corner of the room and decorate it to imitate the experience you want them to imagine. You may also choose to read a short story about the subject on which your attention will be focused. You might ask questions to help children recall similar experiences.
TRANSFER - Explain that you will guide them in an imaginary journey within their body.

OBJECTIVE
The student will be able to focus his mind and attain a sense of inner balance by connecting his body and mind through his imagination.

INPUT & MODELING
1. Motivational activity. Talk to students about the pace of the activity. If they are going to pretend to be a seedling sprouting and beginning to grow, will they move quickly or slowly? Show children how to move slowly when growing into a flower before the actual exercise begins. A book like "Sunflower" of the Watch It Grow series by Barrie Watts is useful to illustrate the message.
2. Explain that students will assume a position. There are a couple positions you may choose to use (Resting postures are good starting points, for example lying on the floor in Sleeping Beauty, if you are using it to calm students after being active or standing in Mountain pose if allowing them to utilize their bodies as part of the experience to stretch their imagination as well as their body. Use your judgment to determine if closing the eyes would be beneficial to the experience.
3. Show them the position they will use for this exercise. In this particular exercise students will begin in Child's pose.
4. Explain that they will listen to you describe an experience and they are to imagine they are part of that experience. Instruct them to keep their eyes closed and to listen. Talking, touching, opening their eyes will ruin the experience.

CHECK FOR UNDERSTANDING
5. Ask students if they have any questions about what they are supposed to do.
6. Answer all questions.

GUIDED PRACTICE
7. Have students begin in Child's pose. Experiment with their ability to keep eyes closed for at least part of the journey.
8. In a calm voice, begin describing an experience. Have them try it 1st in 3 short steps. Begin in child's pose (breathing). You are a seed. Small and green, under the soil. A stem begins to grow, have them lift the upper part of their body. Green and long. Your leaves start to sprout. Reach your arms up. Your stem grows taller – come into a squatting position and slowly rise into a standing position. Your flower blossoms and reaches toward the sun. Spread fingers wide and reach toward the sky.
Practice this 2 or 3 times. If your class can handle the step 9, the longer version, take them through it. Explain that they will need to listen and imagine more before moving. If not save it for them when they are ready to progress.
9. "Imagine your body is a tiny seed planted in the warm earth. There are lots of other tiny seeds planted around you in a beautiful garden full of flowers, shrubs, and trees. It is a warm sunny day and a

light rain is falling. You drink in the water to help you grow. Slowly begin to wiggle your body, very slowly, lift your head, shoulders, and upper body so you are sitting back on your heels. Try to keep your eyes closed and imagine the seed you are has sprouted into a small flower stem. Now bring the palms of your hands flat on the floor and lift your bottom so you are squatting. Now imagine you are beginning to grow into a flower. Your arms are shiny green and your hands are flower petals. Breathe in slowly and begin to straighten your knees as you slowly lift your hands and arms, first out to the side and breathe out reaching your hands overhead as if you are growing toward the sun. Now keep breathing, spread your fingers apart, and reach toward the sky. Now focus your energy on your feet, imagine your feet as roots of the flower growing deeply into the ground, deep into the center of the earth. Feel the warmth of the sun penetrate your flower petals and move through your stem down through your roots, giving you strength and energy. See your roots growing deep into the ground. Imagine the colors of the rich earth, brown, red and gold mixed together as your roots sink deeper and deeper into the center of the earth. Now, bring your palms together, bend to the right and to the left. Breathe in and out and lower your arms down by your sides so you are standing straight and tall. Notice how you feel. Are you happy? Peaceful, Calm? Relaxed? Energized? Balanced? Slowly open your eyes."

CLOSURE
10. Discuss how the experience made the students feel.
11. Give students an outline of the body on paper (See Chapter 7). Tell them to think about how they felt during the exercise. Color in the parts of the body using colors that show how you feel. So if black reminds you of feeling sad and you felt sad use black or if pink reminds you of feeling happy and you felt happy use pink.

INDEPENDENT PRACTICE
Give students suggestions for using imaginary journeys at home. Have pre-schoolers create a picture and tell them to make up an imaginary journey using their picture. They might try to go on their own imaginary journeys before going to bed at night or you might share the activity with parents and suggest they help children go on a journey at bedtime.

EXTENSION
If in a classroom setting, plants seeds and watch them grow. Sticky Fingers - Growing Things by Ting and Neil Morris might serve as a useful reference. See Suggested Materials for resources to enhance Exercises.

Notice the similarity of a few of the following journeys to those listed previously, however: The following have been tailored specifically for dramatic play. The last two have been shortened to quickly calm the energy of younger students.

The Park - Active
Gather children in a large circle. We are going to use our bodies as a group to imitate the things we see in the park, you will listen to me describe the things we see and when I tell you to open your eyes, I'll explain how to work with your group to create what we just saw. Tell them, close your eyes. We are going to imagine we are in the park on a beautiful sunny day. The sky is blue and a light breeze is blowing. First we are going to walk over to the playground. Lets all get on the see saw. Tell children to take the hand of one person sitting next to them. That will be their partner for the see saw. Partners sit across from each other, legs spread, holding hands and stretch back and forth, back and forth. Do this several times. Boy, that was fun! Let's go on the slide now. Keep your same partner, sitting on the ground, face each other, hold hands, put the soles of your feet together, and slowly raise your feet together creating a V. You will both be balancing on your bottom, legs straight, and soles of feet together. Allow children to balance in this position for a while. Ok, I'm ready to go on the swings. Stand with your partner back to back in Mountain pose (leave some space so you are not touching each other), jump your feet apart, now bend forward at your waist and reach through your legs to grab your partners hands. Partners will take turns stretching down toward their feet. When one's head is horizontal, the others are by their feet. Try swinging with your eyes closed; imagine a cool breeze blowing through your hair. Feel the warm energy of the sunrays spray upon you. Listen to the sounds around you. Kids laughing, birds singing, and water from the sprinklers splashing on the pavement. You feel at peace being part of nature. You slowly come to a still position, sit in bell pose and close your eyes. Pay attention to how and what you're feeling. Relax and breathe. Imagine when your open your eyes, you are sitting in the grass surrounded by beautiful red tulips. Breathe in, smell the scent of the flowers. Now move into a large group circle. Keep the circle tight. Everybody places the soles of their feet together; knees are bent and stretched out. Everybody's knees should be touching, if not make the circle smaller. Each person will bring their arms in between their legs under the back of each knee. Try to take the hands of the person on either side. Your legs will come up off the ground and everyone will be trying to balance as a group. When everyone is balanced, see if the group can straighten their legs out to the sides, crossing over their neighbors legs without falling over. Hold the pose for 5 seconds. Slowly release arms first and then legs. Allow children to lie down, feet in the center of the circle in Sleeping Beauty pose. Tell them, you are quiet and peaceful at rest with yourself. Be still and breathe. Slowly open your eyes. Wiggle your fingers and toes.

Bouncing Ball – Active
Gather children in a large circle. Show them how to use body language and facial expression. Talk them through the motions. Actually act out going into a room like the one you are describing. Tell them to imagine, you are in a big, beautiful playroom. The floors are colored brightly with red, yellow, and blue squared flooring. The walls are made of glass so the sun shines through on everything in the room. There are sliding glass doors that lead outside into a large grassy field. The doors are open and you can smell the scent of freshly cut grass. It is a warm spring day and a light breeze passes through the room. You feel the air on your skin. You hear the sound of birds chirping and other children outside laughing and playing. In the middle of the floor are large bouncing balls (the kind with a handle so you can sit on them and hold on). There are balls of every color – pink, blue, orange, yellow, green, purple, and red. You walk over and choose one of the balls. Let all the children gather where the balls would be and have them pick one. Go through the motions of actually sitting on the ball. You can choose any colored

ball you like. You grab hold of the handle and sit on the ball. The balls of your feet are lightly touching the floor. Have students begin to bounce on their imaginary ball. You begin bouncing on the ball, up and down, up and down all around the room. Now it is time to go on an adventure to any place you choose. Maybe you would like to bounce to a playground or an amusement park. Maybe you just want to bounce to a big field. You decide it is your adventure. You bounce out the sliding glass doors to a place where you will have fun and will be able to forget your worries and relax and enjoy yourself. Bring yourself there now and try to imagine all the different sound, sights, and smells. You may even imagine how the experience feels. Have children stop and sit in bell pose. Breathe deeply and relax, I will stay quite for a minute while you breathe and relax. (Pause for about 30 seconds) Now climb off your bouncing ball and lie down in comfortable spot. Tell children to lie down in sleeping beauty pose. Let your whole body relax. Your head… your neck…your shoulders…your arms, hands and fingers… your upper body …your lower body…your legs, feet and toes. Breathe and relax.   Listen as I count back from 5 to 1, when I reach 1 wiggle your fingers and toes and slowly open your eyes.

The Farm - Active
Imagine it is a crisp autumn day. The sun is shining and the air smells sweet, fresh and clean. It is early morning and we are going for a hayride to the apple groves on the farm. I'm Farmer Joe and we are ready to go. Motion for students to climb into the wagon and say, "everybody line up! Now climb into the wagon and sit on a bail of hay". Teacher leads the activity. Have children sit in a semi circle like in a wagon. Tell them," the country is quiet and peaceful". Say, "Listen to the quiet. Look over their there is a vegetable patch. See the tiny country animals sniffing the lettuce. Look at the rabbits, chipmunks, and field mice scurrying about getting ready for winter. Do you feel the breeze against your skin? Oh. The road is bumpy!! Feel how the wagon moves up and down on the dirt road. We're here, at the apple grove, be careful climbing out. (Lead the way). Move slowly, we are going to begin picking apples. Look at all the different apples. There are green apples, yellow apples, and red apples. You choose your favorite color of the three, pick one, and take a bite. (Show them how to take a bite of an imaginary apple). Mmm, the fruit is sweet and juicy. Everybody fill your bag (you lead the action). Ok, lets get back on the wagon and rest on the hay in the wagon. Do you feel the wagon begin to slowly move? Enjoy the ride, breathe, and relax. We are on our way back from where we came. The wagon has stopped, how do you feel?"

The Beach - Active
The teacher is the Captain of a ship. Explain to the children that they are going on an imaginary journey on a ship to spend some time at the beach. The captain says, "all aboard!" Wave children onto the ship. Direct children to sit in pairs in bell pose, side by side in two rows as if sitting on the outer edge of a boat. 'We are going to take a trip to the beach; the beach is a great place to relax and play. We can sit on the beach and look out at the water. Oh, look there it is - we are almost there! Feel the wind in your hair (run your fingers through your hair, encourage children to do the same) and the warmth of the sun of your skin! Feel the boat rock (have children hold feet and rock back and forth) and the water splash on your body. We are here, lets get out and find a place in the sand to put our towels down." Lead the children out of the boat and say "Follow me in a line." Have children make a circle. Act out and say, "Let's lay our towels down and sit in a circle so we can all see each other. Now smooth out your towels. " Sit back, legs straight out in front, hands behind you holding you up (fan pose). "Ok, everybody sit down on your towel, feet in the center of the circle. Put your toes in the sand, ooh it is warm and tingly. Ok, everybody lay down on your backs now in sleeping beauty pose. Now relax and lets all breathe in and out together, slowly. Look up in the sky, what do you see? (Answers: clouds and sun) Look at the

sun, what color is it? (Answers: white, yellow, and orange) How does the sun feel? Now, pretend the sun is like a container of water pouring down from the sky all over your body. It feels warm and refreshing! Now, look at the clouds, what color are the clouds? (Answer: white) Now, pretend the clouds are a beautiful, white blanket that float down from the sky and cover you up. Close your eyes, breathe slowly and deeply, and go to sleep. " Let children rest for about 30 seconds.

The Rainbow Play Express - Active
The teacher is the Conductor on the Rainbow Play Express Choo Choo Train. Explain to children that the Rainbow Play Express is a train that goes to imaginary places in imaginary lands far, far away. All children get in a line and hold onto each other's waists. "All aboard the Rainbow Play Express. Everybody say, " Chug, chug, chug, chug, chug, chug, chug, chug, toot - toot, we are going on Safari to a warm place where all different kinds of animals live in peace. The place is called, Amity Village. Teacher leads children in a large circle around the room. Repeat, Chug, chug, etc. "Pay attention to what you see, look out the window, Oh, look a beautiful tall mountain! Lets stop the train, get out, and explore. Everybody, lets try to be like the Mountain. Instruct children to get into Mountain pose, giving them details, stand tall, and straight like a mountain, arms down by your side. Your head is the top of the mountain and your feet are the base of the mountain. Breathe in and smell the fresh mountain air. Tell children to get back on the train and tell them every time the train stops we will be what we see. Lead the train through Amity Village, stop to see tall trees, a flamingo, a horse, a lion, a dog/wolf a cobra, etc. and lead them through the postures, if animals allow them to make sound and move like the animal, if another part of nature be creative.

Go to an Island With a Buddy – Active
Allow children to choose partners, give them numbers, partner 1 and partner 2. Improvise a scenario - You will probably have to model some positions as your go along the journey.
Ok, boys and girls we are going to get in a boat and row our boat to a fun island where there are lots of sights and fun things to do. Sit on the ground with your partner, spread your legs apart and place the soles of your feet together, take hands and alternate bending forward (Sing Row, Row, Row your Boat). Whew, we are here! My arms are tired from all that rowing. Shake arms out. Coax kids to do what you are doing. What a beautiful island. Lets get out of our boats and onto the island. Have children march in a circle, and then allow the circle to widen and open. The sun is shining brightly, lets become the sun. Face your partner and place your palms together. Raise your hands straight up into the air over head and then out to the side making a circle. All right everybody lets go explore some more. I see a stand where we can rent bicycles. Ok partners, let's get on our bikes, and ride. Face your partner; sit down facing each other, legs outstretched, and soles of feet together. Alternate bending knees, like you are riding a bike. Talk about what you see on the way. I see a bridge up ahead, lets become the bridge. Face your partner, place your hands on each other's shoulders, and begin to bend forward stepping back as your arms and back become flat. Hold and breathe. Ok let's get back on our bikes and ride over that bridge. Let children do the bicycle exercise. Look up a head there is a beautiful fountain; keep pumping until we get to the fountain. We are here. Ok, lets become the fountain. Partners face each other, on their knees, hold hands, and bend backwards. What a beautiful fountains you've become. Are your ready to continue our journey? Let's get back on our bikes. Look up ahead I see a big fence, who can tell me what color that fence is? We are here already. Before we see what is on the other side, maybe we could use our bodies to feel what if might be like to be a fence? Let's try. Face your partner. Partner 1 lift your foot and allow partner two to hold your foot in their hand at hip level. Partner 2 then lifts his opposite foot and partner 1 grabs hold of it at hip level. Partner take hold of each other's free hand and raise it overhead. Oh, look the fence is protecting a beautiful garden. There are many beautiful trees in

the garden. Let's pretend to be a beautiful tree. Partners stand together in tree. Balancing legs on the inside against each other, inside arms wrapped around each other. Outside legs bent, sole of foot on calf or toes resting on floor next to calf, knees turned out and arms overhead. Allow children to have fun and try this on both sides. If partner is too hard to do, let them do it individually. I also see pretty colored flowers all around the trees. Can we try to take the shape of the flowers? Sit on your bottom, facing your partner. Spread your legs and place the soles of your feet together. Hold hand between your legs and each partner lean back a little. Try to raise your feet up together at the same time so you are both balancing on your bottom, feet in the air. Breathe. I see butterflies looking for flowers to rest on. Everybody sit in butterfly. Put your antennae up and rest on your flower. Allow children to rest in this position. Ok, it is time to go home now. Let's get back on our bikes and pedal back to our boat. All children do bike pose with their partner. Ok, we are back, let's get back on the boat. Everybody come into a circle and walk in the circle. Tell them we are going to rest now. Everybody lie down in sleeping beauty pose, feet in the center of the circle. Make the circle big so they can rest comfortably. Have children do some relaxation breathing with soft music playing in the background.

The Aviary – Active
You may choose to bring in pictures of birds for this activity.
Has anybody ever been to an aviary? Does anyone know what an aviary is? (A building for keeping birds). How would you like to visit the aviary now? Ok, I need some imagination. Everybody close your eyes and imagine we are inside a building with lots of trees, plants, and water. The temperature of the building is warm and inviting. We walk over to a pond and inside the pond are ducks. The ducks are swimming and some are waddling on the rocks. Lets use our imagination to become a duck. Have children squat and place their hands under their under arms for wings. Let them walk around in the squatting position, quacking and pretending to be ducks. Tell them to stop, sit in bell pose, and use their imagination again. Now imagine under a shrub is a cute little Roadrunner, picking at some seed. Let all try to imitate the Roadrunner. Instruct children to start on their hands and knees (horse pose). Tell them to bring one foot up between their hands, bending their knee and to straighten the other leg out behind them, curling the toes under to lift the leg off the ground (runners lunge). Children may bob their head to pick at seed. Oh look, there is Mr. pigeon, he looks like he might want to try some seed too. Let see if we can be like the pigeon. From the Roadrunner position, you can easily drop your knee down to the floor and rest on your hip. The foot of the outstretched leg becomes flat on the floor and the leg drops down to the floor (refer to description earlier in book). Head and chest are lifted. Children may coo and flap their wings or bob their head for seed. You may instruct them to stretch their wings out in front and lay their forehead down for a snooze. Allow children to come to a sitting position. Tell them to breathe for a moment. Imagine we walk over to a grassy area and in the grass is a large, fluffy ostrich. Lets pretend to be an ostrich. Have children begin on hands and knees (horse pose), palms flat, fingers spread out and turned in to the center. Your knees are together, with your feet lifted up. You back are flat. Bend your elbows and move your chest toward the ground but don't touch the ground. Let them bob up and down bending at the elbow. Ok, everybody come to your feet now we are going to take a little walk, have children walk in place. Now stand in Mountain pose, imagine in the distance under a tree you see a beautiful, pink Flamingo. I wonder if we could try to balance like the flamingo? Why don't we give it a try? Show them first, and then have children focus on an object on the floor. Instruct them to stretch their wings out to the side and make sure one foot is planted firmly on the ground. Tell them to lift the other leg up behind them (refer to description in book) so their eyes are toward the floor. If children have difficulty with this pose, you may have them try it with a partner holding on to each other's arm. Over time even small children can master this pose. You may have them try it on both sides. Twin Flamingos! Wow, what a great trip to the aviary. Have them sit in bell pose and breathe. What bird did you like the best?

Quiet Imaginary Journey - Use these lying in Sleeping Beauty
Park - Close you eyes. Imagine you are in the park on a beautiful sunny day. The sky is blue. A light breeze is blowing. Pick your favorite ride. Maybe you like the swings, the slide or the teeter-totter - choose the one you like most. Get on and enjoy how you feel as the cool breeze rushes through your hair. Feel the warm energy of the sunrays spray upon you. Listen to the sounds around you. You hear friends laughing, birds singing, and the pitter-patter of water from the sprinklers splashing on the ground. You feel peaceful being part of nature. You slowly come to a still position - How do you feel? What do you feel? Relax and breathe. You are quiet and peaceful at rest with yourself. Be still and breathe. Slowly open your eyes. Wiggle your fingers and toes.

Clouds
Imagine it is a warm sunny day. You walk out of your classroom into a large field. You lie down on a soft, cottony towel in the grassy field. Above you, the sky is blue and full of beautiful white fluffy clouds. Focus on one of the clouds and imagine it turns into a pool of white liquid in a large, light blue pitcher. A tiny fairy tips the pitcher slowly, pouring the liquid over your head and body. As the liquid covers each part of your body, breathe deeply and allow yourself to relax more and more with each exhalation. Relax your head, shoulders, arms, upper body, lower body, legs, and feet. (Pause 10 seconds.) Now see a soft billowy cloud float down, scoop you up, and wrap around you so you feel cozy and warm. It lifts you up into the sky among the other clouds. You feel light as a feather as it carries you higher and higher into the sky above the earth's atmosphere. You are relaxed and calm. The cloud feels like a plush comfortable cushion. Do you feel a sense of freedom? The air smells so fresh and clean. Relax and breathe. (Pause 15 seconds) Your ride is ending as the cloud that carries you slowly descends to the earth. It gently lowers you into your seat in your classroom. You feel your feet flat on the floor beneath you. Pay attention to how and what you feel. (Suggestion Here) Listen for me to count from 5 to 1. When I reach 1 slowly wiggle your toes and fingers and then open your eyes.
Suggestion: Remember the feeling of calm and peace and how you were able to create these feelings whenever you feel excited and need to quiet your energy.

CHAPTER 5

EXPRESS YOURSELF!

CREATIVE DRAMA

Creative Drama means to use the imagination to invent an artistic or intellectual production of human emotion. Engaging children in the process of creative drama promotes a positive self-concept by allowing them freedom to express themselves. When children use the dramatic medium to share ideas they are able to develop and grow on a personal level, as well as an educational level.

When students Rainbow Play they create movement stories as a means of self-expression. They utilize mindful movement postures as a springboard for dramatic action. Involvement in this process is an effective way to cultivate success in the areas of problem solving, language & communications, creativity, social awareness, clarification of values & attitudes, empathy and promoting a positive self-concept. The following lessons may be used to instruct students in the concept of using movement as a form of expression.

ANTICIPATORY SET
FOCUS – The use of sound and movement.
PURPOSE - To utilize the creative process as a means of self-expression.
MOTIVATION - Discuss the concept of making inanimate objects come to life and giving human qualities to things in nature. Relate the concept to children's video programs or cartoon.
TRANSFER: Explain how mindful movement can be used for creative expression by creating movement and sound for each posture.

OBJECTIVE
The student will use his imagination to create sound and movement for still postures.

INPUT AND MODELING
1. Motivational Activity.
2. The teacher will start with a position that lends itself naturally to sound and movement. For example, volcano. Slowly ease into positions that stretch the imagination.
3. Discuss the properties of a volcano. A volcano looks like a mountain except it is open on top. It spits out lava, smoke, and fire. When it is active, it might make a rumbling kind of noise. It is volatile and unpredictable.
4. Have children volunteer sound that a volcano might make.
5. Choose a sound to use and have children stand in the posture making the sound.
6. Have children volunteer movement that a volcano might make.
7. Choose a movement and have children put movement to position without sound.
8. Practice using movement and sound at the same time.
9. Now practice the posture quiet and still.
10. Tell children that you are going to split them into groups and assign them each a (or 2 or 3) position. They must give each position sound and movement. The may not assign the property of speech and the movement must be in place (no leaping across the room). At the pre-school level, this may be done as a whole class activity.
11. Tell them they will have 10 minutes and then they will have to perform for each other.

CHECK FOR UNDERSTANDING
12. Ask students if they have any questions about what they are supposed to do.
13. Listen to and answer all questions.

GUIDED PRACTICE
14. Place children in groups of 4 to 6.
15. Assign them 1 to 3 postures.
16. Give them time to create.
17. Monitor groups to assure they are on task.

CLOSURE
18. Have students show each other the sound and movement they created for their assigned positions. Explain to students that they have the ability to change their own energy throughout the day. At any time of the day they can become the Mountain, even when they feel most like a Volcano.

INDEPENDENT PRACTICE
19. Explain to students that this is a form of exercise they can practice at home when they are full of energy, can't sit still, and need something to do.

EXTENSION
20. Lead a group movement class; utilize still positions with active positions. Bring children to an excited state and back to a calm still state. This lesson helps children gain the ability to control altered states of energy.

Sample Routine

Centering:
Diaphragmatic Breathing

Limbering:
Mountain
1/2 Moon
Symmetrical Stretch - Reach for the Stars
Side Stretch

Standing:
Warrior (R) Triangle (R)
Warrior (L) Triangle (L)
Volcano (quiet, bubbling, erupting)
Tree
Squat

Hands and Knees:
Cat (Meow)
Puppy dog stretch
Lion (Quiet, roar)

Rest:
Child's pose

Back Bend and Forward Bend:
Pigeon (coo, coo)
Fan

Sitting:
Butterfly (quiet sound)
Tortoise (hello)
Diamond
Leg Cradles (Shh, Shh)
Rocking Chair (3X)

Laying Down:
Potato Bug or Candle
Sleeping Beauty - Relaxation

Journey - Park

ANTICIPATORY SET
FOCUS - Body awareness.
PURPOSE - To build flexibility and concentration. To recall information and form mental images.
MOTIVATION - Provide a book or video with nature forms and/or animals. (See Suggested Materials.) You may also choose to use a battery-operated animal, a stuffed animal, a live animal, or other hands on nature forms. Ask children if they ever thought about what it would be like to be an animal or another form of nature (relate it to a mindful movement posture you are using in the lesson). Discuss the physical attributes of the chosen subject.
TRANSFER - Explain that students will bring a posture to life by creating movement for it.

OBJECTIVE
The student will listen and move their body as directed by the teacher.
The student will imagine he/she is the animal.

INPUT AND MODELING
1. Motivational activity.
2. The teacher tells students which posture they will be bringing to life.
3. She asks students to recall the posture. She directs everyone to get into the posture.
4. If anyone has forgotten the posture this will jog his or her memory.
5. Teacher chooses a student to model the activity before working with the entire group.
6. She plays a previously prepared audiotape while students follow the directions to bring the cat posture to life. Use of the audiotape allows the teacher to facilitate the action.

CHECK FOR UNDERSTANDING
7. The teacher asks if there are any questions about what the students are supposed to do.
8. Teacher answers all questions.

GUIDED PRACTICE
9. Teacher instructs all students to get into Cat posture.
10. She describes the actions out loud for the movement activity. Movements may involve levels, direction, tempo, character, and topics. The action should involve the whole body. Students pretend to be the animal or object.
11. The description may be as follows:
The Cat- Students begin in traditional Cat posture. The teacher describes the following action. " You are a lazy white cat peering through the tall green grass. You arch your back high up toward the bright blue sky and lower your head bending it toward your chest. Now lift your head, look straight ahead, and reach your rights paw straight out in front of you. Extend your left hind leg straight out behind you, pause and sniff the air, breathe in and out. Lower your rights paw and left hind leg.
Now, rest in child's pose.

CLOSURE
12. Students may write in journals about their experience or teacher may lead a discussion and write a class journal summarizing the experience. **Variation** - Teacher may choose to close lesson with a silent breathing exercise.

INDEPENDENT PRACTICE
Teacher may suggest that students try this activity at home. They may choose the movements for a given posture on their own. (See Chapter 7)

Variations For Pre-School Students:
CLOSURE
Teacher may lead a discussion and write a class journal summarizing the experience or write a class poem embracing the body awareness activity. **Variations** - Teacher may choose to close lesson with a silent breathing exercise. Teacher may choose to have student create an art piece, for example, a mask of a cat. The next time students practice the activity; they can wear their masks. Some suggestions for Craft books are in the back of the book. A few good books are The Big Book of Paper craft by Usborne and Simple Puppets from Everyday Materials by Barbara MacDonald Buetter. Also, see "Invent Your Own", in the Games for a Quick Stress Break.

ANTICIPATORY SET
FOCUS - Emotions
PURPOSE - To promote awareness and expressions of children's own feelings
MOTIVATION - Refer to one of the books about feelings in the materials section. Read the book and discuss with children how they can tell what someone is feeling by looking at them. Talk to them about how we can show our emotions without speaking. Define the word pantomime for them. Definition: Using actions and expressions without words to show how you feel.
TRANSFER - Ask the students to think of a feeling word and raise their hand when they have one. Choose a child to respond. When the child answers, pantomime the feeling with actions and facial expression.

OBJECTIVE
The student will begin to learn the essence of drama/acting.
The student will loosen up become less inhibited.
The student will gain awareness of his ability to control his behavior when emotions arise. The Student will have fun.

INPUT & MODELING
1. Motivational activity
2. Transfer. Act out a couple responses that children offer and then let them know it is going to be their turn next.
3. Tell them you will call out a feeling word and they are all supposed to act out each feeling. This is done as a group. It may help to begin with the actions they gave you to act out. If you see a child pantomiming a feeling particularly well or if a particular child is naturally dramatic in manner, you may consider having the other children observe him. Below are some feeling words and their meaning.

CHECK FOR UNDERSTANDING
4. Ask children if they know what they are supposed to do. Have them repeat it back to you.

GUIDED PRACTICE
5. Teacher begins by calling out words one at a time and allowing children to pantomime as a group.
6. After watching the whole group pantomime a feeling, you may ask one half of the students to show the other half and alternate. Observing helps to motivate students.

ANGRY - A feeling of displeasure.
SAD - Having low spirits or showing sorrow.
SCARED - Filled with fear or a sudden panic.
COMPASSIONATE - Feeling sad for the suffering of another accompanied by an urge to help.
JEALOUS - Watchful or suspicious of another's influence. A strong urge to possess someone else's property.
HAPPY - A feeling of great pleasure or contentment.
ANXIOUS - An uneasy mind, worried.
FRUSTRATED - A feeling of defeat resulting from the prevention of achieving one's goal.
GUILTY - A painful feeling resulting from the belief that one has done wrong.
HURT - Mental pain or wounded feelings.
MISCHIEVOUS - Full of tricks, naughty.
PUZZLED - Confused, uncertain, or bewildered.
RELIEVED - Free from discomfort or anxiety.
SATISFIED - Content or free from doubt.
DISAPPOINTED - Unsatisfied.
EXHAUSTED - Tired, weary, and drained. Completely used up.
7. This activity can be done with a variety of adjectives and verbs. You do not have to limit it to feelings. For example, COLD, CLUMSY, HOT, GRACEFUL, SICK, TIRED, ETC.

CLOSURE
Have children use their relaxation breathing to calm. Allow them to discuss the experience.

INDEPENDENT PRACTICE
Tell children that they can practice this at home with their family or friends.

EXTENSION
Freeze and bring to life activity.

ANTICIPATORY SET
FOCUS - To freely express oneself in a healthy manner through a movement story.
PURPOSE - To develop a positive self-concept and grow personally, as well as, educationally.
MOTIVATION - Show students a picture book without words or one with very few words. Have students tell you about the story. (May also use a dance video. See Suggested Materials for resources).
TRANSFER - Explain to students that they are going to create a story with their bodies. Each part of the story will be like the pictures in the book.

OBJECTIVE
The student will use his imagination to invent a story that artistically expresses his feelings and emotions using mindful movement postures as a base for movement.

INPUT AND MODELING
1. Motivational Activity.
2. The teacher explains that the students will first go an imaginary journey or will participate in a body awareness activity (this has previously been experienced by all students in class).
3. When the journey or activity is complete, students record their feelings in their journal or the teacher may ask children to write a descriptive poem or paragraph that expresses how they felt during the

exercise. Teacher instructs students to think about which postures best symbolize the feelings they experienced.

4. Teacher may show students a videotape of her own movement-based story. She explains how students are going to work in a group to combine all their feelings together and create a group story. For example, if a student writes he felt energized, he might choose half moon posture to symbolize energy. If he wrote about feeling anger, he might strike Lion pose. A student may move into several postures to express each feeling experienced. The creative movement group will assemble all their postures together as an expression of their feelings. If students are comfortable, they may integrate interpretive movement, words or sound as they move in and out of postures using the flow of movement as a cathartic release.

CHECK FOR UNDERSTANDING
5. Ask students if they have any questions about what they are expected to do.
6. Listen to and answer all questions.

GUIDED PRACTICE
7. Students may choose their own groups. However, have a set number of students predetermined for each group so that no one is left without a group. If this is not possible, assign students to groups you have chosen.
8. Teacher monitors each group to assure they are on task.

CLOSURE
9. Students act out entire story within the group. Teacher observes.

INDEPENDENT PRACTICE
Students may create individual movement stories in a class center. If teacher is comfortable she may have groups work in the center. (See Chapter 7)

EXTENSION
If groups are comfortable they may present story for other groups in the class.

Variations For Pre-School Students:

INPUT AND MODELING
1. Motivational Activity.
2. The teacher explains that the students will first have an imaginary journey experience (this has previously been experienced by all students in class). You may also use a body awareness activity to stimulate feelings for a class poem.
3. When the imaginary journey session is complete, students record their feelings as a class. Teacher helps students create a short poem, paragraph, or story with the feelings. Teacher instructs students to think about which postures best symbolize the feelings they experienced during the exercise. For example, "Billy said he felt happy, what posture would you pick to show me you felt happy?" Focus on a few feeling words and postures.
4. Teacher explains how we are going to work in a group to combine all their feelings together and create a group story. For example, if a student said he felt energized, the group might choose half moon posture to symbolize energy. If someone talked about feeling anger, the group might strike Lion pose. The group may string together several postures to express each feeling experienced during a session. The creative movement group will assemble all their postures together as an expression of their feelings. The teachers may act as a narrator to guide students through the movement. If students are comfortable, they may integrate interpretive movement, words or sound as they move in and out of postures using movement as a cathartic release.

CHECK FOR UNDERSTANDING
5. Ask students if they have any questions about what they are expected to do.
6. Listen to and answer all questions.

GUIDED PRACTICE
7. At the pre-school level, the teacher leads the discussion. The whole group works together to create their story or the teacher may use a story like The Billy Goats Gruff (See Chapter 7) the first couple times to help children get the idea. Teacher closely monitors the group.

CLOSURE
9. Students act out entire story within the group. Teacher may choose to do a follow-up art activity. Students may make masks to use during their performance or puppets that can be utilized at the same time. While some are using their bodies to perform, other students are using puppets. A good craft book is Crafty Puppets by Thomasina Smith. See the back of the book for more suggestions.

INDEPENDENT PRACTICE
Students may create masks and puppets.

EXTENSION
Teacher may choose to have students perform for their parents.

Movement Based Activities

Movement Story - In a movement based story, students express their feelings through the use of postures. When working with younger students, a teacher might want to use a traditional story for beginning exercises (The Three Little Pigs, Billy Goats Gruff). If she chooses this route, she will need to read the story and edit it into a brief version. She might choose to have all the students acting in unison or she might assign characters to various groups of students or individual students. Each group of students would have a different character focus and would freely strike postures to explore character feelings during the narration. Students stay in a particular posture until the feeling changes. If students get tired they may release into mountain pose. (Sample revised story page 128- Appendix)
A teacher might also create an original movement story. Students would decide which postures best interpret the feelings being expressed by the characters and develop a creative movement story together as a class or in small groups.

Movement Story - When working with older students, begin with an imaginary journey session to help students get in touch with their feelings through imaginary journey. When the exercise is complete, students write their feelings in their journals. Afterwards, they communicate those feelings through the use of movement. For example, if a student writes he felt energized, he might choose Half Moon posture to symbolize energy. If he wrote about feeling anger, he might strike Lion pose. A student might move into several postures to express each feeling experienced during an imaginary journey session. The creative movement group would assemble all their postures together as an expression of their feelings. If students are comfortable, they may integrate words or sound as they move in and out of postures using creative movement as a cathartic release.

ANTICIPATORY SET
FOCUS - To cultivate values and attitudes for living.
PURPOSE - To involve students in the dramatic process to help them clarify and express their values and attitudes.
MOTIVATION - Read a short picture book about a value such as responsibility, compassion, etc. When story is complete, discuss the concepts in the book. (See "10 Steps For Getting Along With Others" under Guided Practice.)

OBJECTIVE
To define values and attitudes.
The student will use writing and role-play to creatively express his or her self.
The student will use his imagination to create a skit that conceptualizes a given value and use it to express himself through role-play.

TRANSFER
Explain to students that they are going to write their own stories in a script format. Tell them how writing is often best when it flows easily, just like the way you talk. This is different then proper writing because we don't worry about spelling and punctuation so long as the writer is able to read it aloud. Discuss the parts of a script.

1. The Characters and Narrator.
2. The opening situation or setting.
3. The complications or problems.

4. The plot or crisis.
5. The resolution.

INPUT AND MODELING
1. Copy the following script for use on the overhead projector (See Reproducibles)

Narrator: TWO FRIENDS, LISA AND JODY, WERE SITTING IN CLASS TAKING A TEST. JODY, WHO USUALLY DOES WELL, HADN'T STUDIED. JODY DIDN'T KNOW THE ANSWER TO SOME QUESTIONS SO SHE LOOKED AT LISA'S TEST TO GET THE ANSWERS. WHEN TIME WAS UP THE TEACHER COLLECTED THE TESTS. THE TEACHER ASKED LISA AND JODY TO STAY AFTER CLASS THE NEXT DAY.

Teacher: "WILL YOU PLEASE STAY AFTER CLASS?"

Narrator: HE PULLED THEIR TESTS OUT.

Teacher: "YOUR ANSWERS ARE IDENTICAL, I WAS WONDERING IF ONE OF YOU HAS BEEN CHEATING?"

Narrator: JODY HAD ALWAYS DONE WELL IN THE PAST. BOTH GIRLS DENIED CHEATING SO HE BELIEVED JODY MUST HAVE BEEN TELLING THE TRUTH. HE PUNISHED LISA. LISA WAS ANGRY AND CONFRONTED JODY.

Lisa: "DID YOU COPY OFF ME?"

Narrator: JODY ADMITTED SHE DID CHEAT BUT WAS AFRAID TO TELL THE TRUTH.

Explain to students that they should give their characters things to say rather then just narrate the story because they are going to be acting these stores out for each other.

CHECK FOR UNDERSTANDING
2. Ask students if they understand what they are supposed to do?
3. Listen to and answer all questions.

GUIDED PRACTICE
4. Use 10 Steps For Getting Along With Others for script themes.
5. Tell them to keep it to one page with at least 2 characters in the story. Explain when they are finished, we will read them aloud and vote on them to see which we will act out.
6. Students begin to write.
7. Students read stories aloud.
8. Students vote.
9. Break students into cooperative groups. Allow them to cooperatively work on skits. Facilitate by moving from group to group.

CLOSURE
10. Allow Students to role-play skits for each other.
11. Discuss what they learned.

INDEPENDENT PRACTICE
12. Students write skits in centers about VALUE/ATTITUDE words of the week or month.

EXTENSION
13. Students perform for parents.

BOOKS FOR CONSIDERATION
The following books explain concepts such as:
Empathy - When my friend feels sad, I feel sad
Compassion - When my friend is in trouble, I feel sorry he is hurting and want to help him
Respect - How do I show consideration for others?
Cooperation - Working with others for shared interests
Responsibility - Are others able to depend on me to do what I say I will do?
Citizenship - What kind of behaviors show I am a citizen of my school? Show the connection between these concepts and the 10 Steps.

Character Education Series by Lucia Raatma
Titles: Caring, Consideration, Friendliness, Honesty, Peacefulness, Respect, Responsibility, Tolerance.

Do The Right Thing Series by Shelagh Canning
Titles: Caring, Friendship, Honesty, Kindness, Manners, Sharing

Arthur's Computer Disaster by Marc Brown - trust

Voices of the Heart by Ed Young - This book defines "character" words.

Glenna's Seeds by Nancy Edwards - kindness/citizenship

The Other Side by Jacqueline Woodson - friendship/respect

American Too by Ted Lewin - loyalty/citizenship

When I Am Old With You by Angela Johnson - respect/empathy

Raising Yoder's Barn by Jane Yolen - cooperation/citizenship/empathy/compassion

Variation For Pre-School Students:

ANTICIPATORY SET
FOCUS – Values and Attitudes
PURPOSE - To promote awareness of character development from learning about values and attitudes.
MOTIVATION - Read the children a book about a character trait. Talk to children about the concept of character, explain that it is the kind of person you are. Use the 10 Steps as a guide for your themes. Respect, peace, honesty, self-control, patience, cleanliness, attitude, taking care of yourself. A good series is Sandcastle-Building Character, which covers Responsibility, respect, honesty, citizenship, fairness, and caring.
TRANSFER - Ask how they practice the character trait you've read about to them in their own lives. Allow different children to give answers and talk about those answers.

OBJECTIVE
The student will know what character is and what traits build strong character.
The student will be able to give examples of how he/she exhibits different character traits.

INPUT & MODELING
1. Motivational Activity. (This lesson may be used periodically to learn about different traits)
2. After you have received a variety of answers, tell each child that you want them to try and think of 2 or 4 ways they've just heard of how they might exhibit the trait.
3. Explain that you are going to give them a sheet of paper and they are going to fold it in half or in fours depending on the number of responses you want. You will stand in front and fold yours while they are folding theirs.
4. In the sections of the paper they will draw a picture that shows the different ways they exhibit the trait.
5. Fold a piece of paper and show they what you mean.

CHECK FOR UNDERSTANDING
1. Ask them what they are going to do when they get the paper.
    a. Watch you fold your paper and fold theirs the same way.
    b. Draw a picture in each section that shows the way they exhibit the trait.

GUIDED PRACTICE
1. Hand out the paper. Show students how to fold the paper.
2. Remind them to think of 2 ways they exhibit the trait.
3. Tell them to draw the different ways in each section.

CLOSURE
1. Show -n- Tell - Have children volunteer to share their pictures in front of the other kids and explain the different ways to exhibit the trait.

INDEPENDENT PRACTICE
Tell the child when he/she gets home to do something that exhibits the trait. For example, if the trait is responsibility, tell the child to do something responsible when they go home today.

EXTENSION
Make puppets. Have children use their pictures to help them remember and act out the example of how they exhibit the trait. This could be done in pairs. You could also try this with masks and have them act it out.

BOOKS FOR CONSIDERATION AT THE PRE-SCHOOL LEVEL

Sandcastle Character Education Series: I am Responsible, Honest, A Good Citizen, Respectful, Caring, Fair. Good series for pre-school. Check for Age-appropriateness.

Do The Right Thing Series by Shelagh Canning
Titles: Caring, Friendship, Honesty, Kindness, Manners, Sharing

A Duck So Small by Elizabeth Holstien - group acceptance

The Loudness of Sam by Janes Proimos - expressing feelings

Arthur's Computer Disaster by Marc Brown - trust

Voices of the Heart by Ed Young - This book defines "character" words

Glenna's Seeds by Nancy Edwards - kindness/citizenship

The Other Side by Jacqueline Woodson - friendship/respect

American Too by Ted Lewin - loyalty/citizenship

When I Am Old with You by Angela Johnson - respect/empathy

CHAPTER 6

ENRICHMENT

SENSORY ENHANCEMENT

Relaxation techniques such as imaginary journey work, mindful movement, focused awareness exercises; using music, aromatherapy, and color to create a more relaxing atmosphere or stimulate a mood change may enhance deep breathing and creative movement. A calming oil may be diffused during academic testing to soothe nerves or the teacher might choose an essential oil that promotes relaxation while students engage in an exercise. When students enter the room in the morning she may choose peaceful music to play softly in the background. A room or bulletin board may be decorated with specific colors to affect various moods or the teacher may describe calming colors when using imaginary journeywork. Any sensory enhancement may be used through out the course of the academic day. The teacher has greater ability to affect the mood in her classroom using sensory enhancers as management tools. Below is a list of colors and the energy created when using these colors.

COLOR AND ENERGY

Red	excitement
Orange	warm-hearted
Yellow	alert/clear thinking
Green	self-acceptance
Blue	calming/peaceful
Black	self-discipline
White	hope
Gold	uplifting/forgiveness
Silver	tranquility

When trying to effect a mood change diffuse the following oils separately or experiment with different aromas by blending two oils together.

ESSENTIAL OILS AS MOOD ENHANCERS

Anxiety	Bergamot
	Lavender
Concentration	Orange
	Sandalwood
Anger	Roman Chamomile
	Ylang Ylang
Balance	Geranium
	Bergamot

See the Resources section for books on aromatherapy and color. See Suggested Materials for musical audio references.

TRY RAINBOW PLAY AS AN EXTENSION TO A SUBJECT BASED LESSON

Interpretive Movement using Literature

History or Language Arts
After reading a historical or language arts story, students create interpretive movement stories as a means to understand and emphasize with the characters. Students work in small groups. They use mindful movement postures, free movement, language, sound, and gestures to depict the emotion in a story or interpret a relationship between characters.
(Follow lesson plan for movement based activities.)

Invent your Own

Science
Many of the postures are named for animals and other forms of nature. Have students think of some that are not already in use. Students invent their own postures using animals and other forms of nature as inspiration.

The following is a list of possibilities:
bear, dragon, elephant, fox, fish, giraffe, horse, kangaroo, lamb, rabbit, penguin,
wind, lightening, thunder, earthquake, gravity, tornado, flower, ocean, rock.

GAMES FOR A QUICK FIX STRESS BREAK

When students are familiar with postures, the following games make concentration fun for little ones.

Simon Says - Example: Simon says be the Cobra or Simon says be the Pigeon. If a students does the wrong posture or moves into posture without Simon's permission, they rest in Child's pose or choose a posture that expresses their feelings in that moment. Instruct students to only hold a posture as long as is comfortable. When they are ready to rest, they assume Child's pose until the game is over.

Follow the Leader - Students take turns leading each other through mindful movement postures. (This game can be used as a form of behavior modification by choosing students who have the most problematic behaviors as the leader).

Freeze - Teacher beats a drum as children walk around a designated area. When the teacher stops beating, students must move into a mindful movement posture. They must stay in the posture until the drumbeat begins again.

Guess Again! - One student assumes a posture while others guess the name of that posture. The person who guesses correctly first, takes a turn. If the guessing takes a long time the student may rest in Mountain pose.

Invent your Own - Many mindful movement postures are named for animals and other forms of nature. Have students think of some that are not already in use. Students invent their own yoga postures using animals and other forms of nature as inspiration. The following is a list of possibilities. bear, dragon, elephant, fox, fish, giraffe, kangaroo, lamb, rabbit, penguin, wind, lightening, thunder, earthquake, gravity, tornado, flower, ocean, rock.
Below are descriptions to stimulate creativity. Create postures and vote on your favorite posture. Write a class poem for your animal. Make masks for the animal. Then put action to your poem. Let children act out while you recite the poem. Play mood music in the background. This may also be an extension of a body awareness activity.

A good book for this activity is, <u>Amazing Animal Alphabet with Fantastic Flaps</u> by Richard Edwards.

Bear - Large, fierce, growls
Elephant - Giant, wide, trumpeting
Fish - Flexible, cold blooded, slippery
Kangaroo - Leaping, strong, large
Rabbit - Soft, furry, long ears
Wind - Strong, fast moving, air
Thunder - Loud, booming, sound
Gravity - Heavy, constant, anchor
Flower - Colored, petals, blossom
Rock - Large, strong, stone

Dragon - Scaly, mysterious, fire breathing
Fox - Small, sly, wild
Giraffe - Tall, long, quiet
Lamb - Gentle, innocent, young
Penguin - Stiff, web footed, bird
Lightening - Bright, electric, flash
Earthquake - Shifting, shaking, earth
Tornado - Rapid, whirling, funnel
Ocean - Great, flowing, water

CHAPTER 7

STANDARDS FOR BEHAVIOR

TEN STEPS FOR GETTING ALONG WITH OTHERS

1. Respect yourself and others. Treat others the same way you would like to be treated, show others consideration, be courteous and avoid being intrusive.

2. Live peacefully. Practice non-violent behavior in every part of your life. If you start thinking mean spirited things, try to focus on more positive thoughts, don't use mean words or violent actions. Surround yourself with loving, caring people.

3. Tell the truth. Avoid being dishonest. Don't do things that you will be tempted to lie about to avoid getting into trouble.

4. Don't steal. Be satisfied with what you have and accept when you can't have something. Don't allow yourself to be greedy. Separate what you want from needing things and/or people.

5. Master self-discipline. Make an effort to do things for periods of time. Don't give into to every urge.

6. Be content. Cultivate a calm attitude. Don't allow yourself to become anxious over what you think you should have or where you should be in your life. Accept where you are in the moment.

7. Practice cleanliness. Have good hygiene; keep living space clean, wash food, etc.

8. Practice self-study. Get know yourself. Contemplate about who you are, what you feel, how you think, if any part of your self may be improved upon and how to do what's necessary to live consciously.

9. Practice thinking positively. Contemplate about what goodness is and think about the meaning of love.

10. Practice mindful movement and breathing exercises. This will help you calm your senses and focus your mind. Move slowly and thoughtfully, listen to your body, and pay attention to your feelings. Balance your physical and mental body.

Utilize Bell pose as a disciplined seated position when practicing activities. When making transitions from one activity to the next, use melodic sounds to signal children that it is time to make a change. For example, a harmonica or flute like instrument. Reinforce positive behaviors and redirect negative behaviors. Show children how to integrate Rainbow Play techniques into every day living situations and give them the opportunity to express their ideas (See Tips For Transfer section, Independent Practice and Extension section of lesson plans for ideas). Review the steps for getting along with others. Discuss each one thoroughly. Focus on each step over a 10 week or 10 month period. Have children journal about each step and how it relates to them in their own life. As a classroom, create rules based on these standards. This interaction will allow the classroom to participate in establishing rules and regulations for responding to behavior in the classroom. Allowing students to take part in this process creates a sense of student ownership.

Dealing with Difficult Behavior
If when working on group activities, a student continually misbehaves try for a moment to actually focus on that behavior. Tell the child to do it more, have the other children join in on the behavior. Then try to gently sway the children back to the desired activity. Try using cooperative discipline techniques to uphold the classroom rules (See below).

Cooperative Discipline Game
This game is used through out the day in combination with Rainbow Play to uphold classroom behavior. Arrange classroom desks in tables. Each table is considered a team. Choose a team captain for each team. Allow students to name their team. Keep the team names and points scored in a highly visible place. Team members receive points for being responsible. For example, if four out of five students from a team bring in homework, the team gets 4 points; no point is received for the child who did not bring in his homework. You may also choose to add points when students exhibit exemplary behavior. For example, stepping back and using relaxation breathing before responding in a volatile situation. At the end of the week, points are counted, the team with the highest score wins. Place a ceiling on the number of points. For example, students should try to stay within 20 points. Give incentives. For example, if all teams reach 20 points, double the reward. If a student is consistently holding back his team you may want to consider having him pulled out? He must earn his way back on to a team. The winning team receives a reward. Classroom jobs might be a motivational reward for lower level students. Free time might be a motivator for higher-level students. Use rewards that you are comfortable integrating into your classroom environment. It is important to change teams at least once a month. Every two weeks is more desirable. It is important for the teacher to be sensitive to students with extenuating circumstances. For instance, if a particular child continually comes to class without homework due to circumstances beyond his control, the teacher might want to find ways to help that child.

CONFLICT RESOLUTION
When conflicts ensue between students, have them practice this exercise:

Students are given time to work disagreement out with a peer mediator present. They use the following script.

1st. Person: I feel _____ when you _____.
2nd. Person: If I'm hearing your correctly, you feel _____ when I _____.
1st. Person: If the response mirrors what he says, he continues with the exercise. If it does not mirror what he said, he repeats what he initially said till the person gets it correct.

The peer mediator listens as an objective 3rd party and helps facilitate conversation.

1st. Person: I need you to _____.
2nd. Person: If I hear you correctly, you need me to _____.
1st. Person: If the response mirrors what he says, he continues with the exercise. If it does not mirror what he said, he repeats what he initially said till the person gets it correct.

The 2nd Person now has the opportunity to express what he feels and needs. Once they both have expressed themselves they may try to compromise if one is necessary.

SUGGESTIONS FOR INTEGRATING RAINBOW PLAY INTO THE DAY

BREAKING IT UP!
IN THE MORNING DURING BELL WORK TIME (20 minutes)
1. Have students begin the day with a breathing exercise.
2. Have students focus on How They Would Like The Day To Be. You may want to refer to "10 Steps" for ideas.
Write on blackboard, "Just for today..." Students complete the sentence with an affirmation that is age appropriate.
Primary grades might have very simplistic affirmations. I will not tattle, I will keep my hands to myself; I will be kind to my classmates.
Middle and upper grades might have more complex affirmations. I love and approve of myself. I am worthwhile. I am important.
(See the back of the book for more affirmations.)
3. Instruct students to focus on it first (1 - 3 minutes is sufficient. Longer, with older students, if you have the time.) Next, have students write about it in their journals or you might instruct them to express themselves artistically.

AFTER LUNCH (10 minutes)
1. Lead students in an imaginary journey exercise.
2. Instruct them to write their feelings in their journal.

END OF THE DAY (Time will vary)
1. If time permits, have students work in groups to create a movement story.
2. If you haven't the time, have students strike a posture that best explores how they felt during the morning or afternoon session or at that very moment. You may choose to instruct students to assume a posture, and then guide a brief body awareness exercise.

Pre-school Variation: SUGGESTIONS INTEGRATING RAINBOW PLAY ACTIVITIES

Sample 1
1. Use the beanbag toss to learn student's names.
2. Play some lively music and have children try to keep a balloon in the air for about a minute or so without letting it touch the ground.
3. Lead students through a group exercise. Focusing on several postures and bringing them to life through movement.
4. Lead students through a Focusesd Awareness activity.
5. Have students breathe deeply for a few seconds while lying in sleeping beauty.

Sample 2
Have students focus on How They Would Like The Day To Be. You may want to refer to "10 Steps" for ideas.
Tell students, "Just for today..." Students complete the sentence with an affirmation that is age appropriate. Pre-school will have very simplistic affirmations. I will not tattle, I will keep my hands to myself; I will be kind to my classmates. (See the back of the book for more affirmations.)
Have Children sit in bell pose and breathe for a few seconds; you may beat a drum in the background. Tell them to think of a posture that expresses their affirmation. For example, Butterfly pose might be

good for I will not tattle because it is a quiet pose. Mountain pose might be good for I will keep my hands to myself because your hands are down by your side.
Talk about their ideas. You may lead a group exercise starting off with the postures they picked.
Practice a group imaginary journey.
Have students draw a picture of their favorite part of the journey.

ENVIRONMENTAL ENHANCEMENTS
1. Aromatherapy is an option for calming students. An air diffuser works best with essential oils. Try this blend mixed in sweet almond oil.
Lavender - 4 drops
Roman chamomile - 1 drop
Lemon - 1 drop
2. Decorate the room in blue to bring a sense of calm to students.
3. Play classical or new age music to foster relaxation.

HAVE A CHUNK OF TIME?
1. Begin with a resting posture (Mountain, Bell, Sleeping Beauty or seated upright in a chair) coupled with an imaginary journey.
2. Practice some postures. Keep the movement flowing.
3. End the practice with students lying on the floor or in a comfortable position.   Lead an imaginary journey meant for relaxation.
4. Instruct students to think about what emotions or feelings came up for them during this exercise. Have students write in their journals.
5. When students are done writing, allow them to work in groups to create movement stories.

AFFIRMATIONS

May be used to set the tone in the morning. Teacher may write one on the board, have students breathe and concentrate on the affirmation and then journal about what it means to them.

I LOVE MYSELF.
    I APPROVE OF MYSELF.
        I AM WORTHWHILE.
            I ACCEPT MYSELF.
                I AM PEACEFUL.
                      MY FEELINGS ARE ACCEPTABLE AND NORMAL.

I AM JOYFUL.
    I AM FREE.
        I CALM MY THOUGHTS.
        I AM SERENE.
            I AM FREE OF IRRITATION.
            ALL IS WELL.

I RESPECT OTHERS FREEDOM TO BE WHO THEY ARE.
    I APPRECIATE MYSELF.
        I ALLOW MY MIND TO RELAX.
        I ALLOW MY MIND TO BE PEACEFUL.
        I LOVE LIFE.
            I AM FILLED WITH ENERGY AND JOY FOR LIVING.

REPRODUCIBLES

CHAPTER 1-WORKSHEET

CHAPTER 1-WORKSHEET

DIRECTIONS: Below are 2 outlines of the human body. Draw a balloon to represent the diaphragm where it is located in the body. On the first outline show what the diaphragm looks like when breathing in and on the second outline show what the diaphragm looks like when releasing the breath.

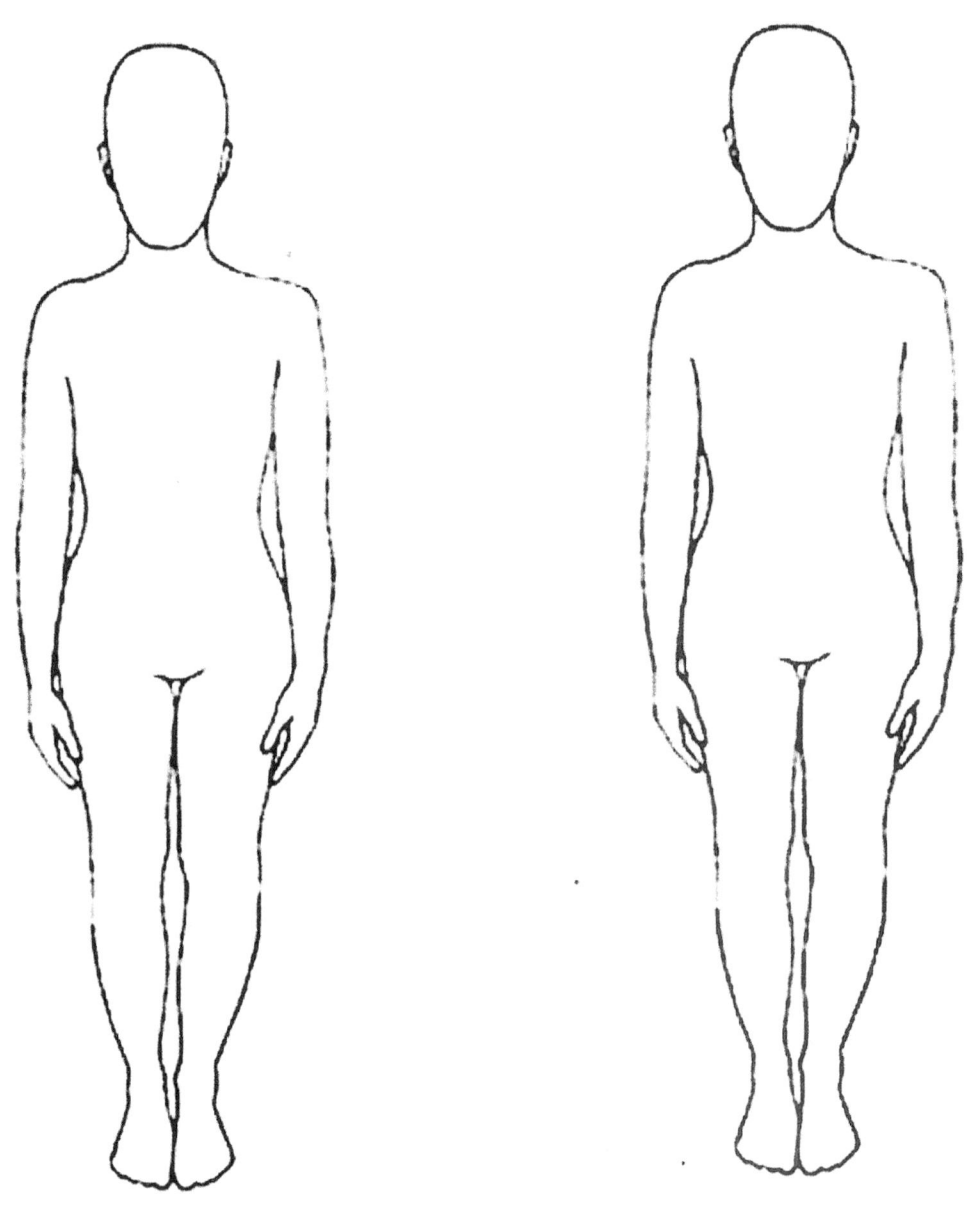

CHAPTER 1 WORKSHEETS

DIRECTIONS: Discuss the feeling word with the students. Talk to them about why they become angry. What are some things that bring up angry feelings for them? Have them think of a situation during the week when they may have felt that way. Have them recall where they notice changes in their body when they feel that way. Have them color in the image of the body showing where they feel the changes in their body (Chapter 4 Worksheet). Tell them to use colors that show their feelings. Below are a list of feeling words and their definitions.

ANGRY - A feeling of displeasure.
SAD - Having low spirits or showing sorrow.
SCARED - Filled with fear or a sudden panic.
COMPASSIONATE - Feeling sad for the suffering of another accompanied by an urge to help.
JEALOUS - Watchful or suspicious of another's influence. A strong urge to possess someone else's property.
HAPPY - A feeling of great pleasure or contentment.
ANXIOUS - An uneasy mind, worried.
FRUSTRATED - A feeling of defeat resulting from the prevention of achieving one's goal.
GUILTY - A painful feeling resulting from the belief that one has done wrong.
HURT - Mental pain or wounded feelings.
MISCHIEVOUS - Full of tricks, naughty.
PUZZLED - Confused, uncertain, or bewildered.
RELIEVED - Free from discomfort or anxiety.
SATISFIED - Content or free from doubt.
DISAPPOINTED - Unsatisfied.
EXHAUSTED - Tired, weary, and drained. Completely used up.

CHAPTER 1- WORKSHEET

DIRECTIONS: Read the word and its definition. Think of a situation during the week when you felt that way. Recall your body sensations when you realized what you were feeling. Draw a picture of yourself that shows the physical changes in your body. You may also write a sentence to explain the picture.

ANGRY- A feeling of displeasure.

DIRECTIONS: Read the word and its definition. Think of a situation during the week when you felt that way. Recall your body sensations when you realized what you were feeling. Draw a picture of yourself that shows the physical changes in your body. You may also write a sentence to explain the picture.

SAD - Having low spirits or showing sorrow.

DIRECTIONS: Read the word and its definition. Think of a situation during the week when you felt that way. Recall your body sensations when you realized what you were feeling. Draw a picture of yourself that shows the physical changes in your body. You may also write a sentence to explain the picture.

SCARED - Filled with fear or a sudden panic.

DIRECTIONS: Read the word and its definition. Think of a situation during the week when you felt that way. Recall your body sensations when you realized what you were feeling. Draw a picture of yourself that shows the physical changes in your body. You may also write a sentence to explain the picture.

COMPASSIONATE - Feeling sad for the suffering of another accompanied by an urge to help.

DIRECTIONS: Read the word and its definition. Think of a situation during the week when you felt that way. Recall your body sensations when you realized what you were feeling. Draw a picture of yourself that shows the physical changes in your body. You may also write a sentence to explain the picture.

JEALOUS - Watchful or suspicious of another's influence. A strong urge to possess someone else's property.

DIRECTIONS: Read the word and its definition. Think of a situation during the week when you felt that way. Recall your body sensations when you realized what you were feeling. Draw a picture of yourself that shows the physical changes in your body. You may also write a sentence to explain the picture.

HAPPY - A feeling of great pleasure or contentment.

DIRECTIONS: Read the word and its definition. Think of a situation during the week when you felt that way. Recall your body sensations when you realized what you were feeling. Draw a picture of yourself that shows the physical changes in your body. You may also write a sentence to explain the picture.

ANXIOUS - An uneasy mind, worried.

DIRECTIONS: Read the word and its definition. Think of a situation during the week when you felt that way. Recall your body sensations when you realized what you were feeling. Draw a picture of yourself that shows the physical changes in your body. You may also write a sentence to explain the picture.

FRUSTRATED - A feeling of defeat resulting from the prevention of achieving one's goal.

DIRECTIONS: Read the word and its definition. Think of a situation during the week when you felt that way. Recall your body sensations when you realized what you were feeling. Draw a picture of yourself that shows the physical changes in your body. You may also write a sentence to explain the picture.

GUILTY - A painful feeling resulting from the belief that one has done wrong.

DIRECTIONS: Read the word and its definition. Think of a situation during the week when you felt that way. Recall your body sensations when you realized what you were feeling. Draw a picture of yourself that shows the physical changes in your body. You may also write a sentence to explain the picture.

HURT - Mental pain or wounded feelings.

DIRECTIONS: Read the word and its definition. Think of a situation during the week when you felt that way. Recall your body sensations when you realized what you were feeling. Draw a picture of yourself that shows the physical changes in your body. You may also write a sentence to explain the picture.

MISCHIEVOUS - Full of tricks, naughty.

DIRECTIONS: Read the word and its definition. Think of a situation during the week when you felt that way. Recall your body sensations when you realized what you were feeling. Draw a picture of yourself that shows the physical changes in your body. You may also write a sentence to explain the picture.

PUZZLED - Confused, uncertain, or bewildered.

DIRECTIONS: Read the word and its definition. Think of a situation during the week when you felt that way. Recall your body sensations when you realized what you were feeling. Draw a picture of yourself that shows the physical changes in your body. You may also write a sentence to explain the picture.

RELIEVED - Free from discomfort or anxiety.

DIRECTIONS: Read the word and its definition. Think of a situation during the week when you felt that way. Recall your body sensations when you realized what you were feeling. Draw a picture of yourself that shows the physical changes in your body. You may also write a sentence to explain the picture.

SATISFIED - Content or free from doubt.

DIRECTIONS: Read the word and its definition. Think of a situation during the week when you felt that way. Recall your body sensations when you realized what you were feeling. Draw a picture of yourself that shows the physical changes in your body. You may also write a sentence to explain the picture.

DISAPPOINTED - Unsatisfied.

DIRECTIONS: Read the word and its definition. Think of a situation during the week when you felt that way. Recall your body sensations when you realized what you were feeling. Draw a picture of yourself that shows the physical changes in your body. You may also write a sentence to explain the picture.

EXHAUSTED - Tired, weary, and drained. Completely used up.

CHAPTER 2-WORKSHEET

Mindful Movement Routines

Routine 1

Breathe	30 sec.

Seated Lion
Standing Mountain
Standing Volcano
Standing Cat
Standing Cobra
Standing Peanut Butter & Jelly
Standing Half Moon
Standing Tree
Seated Twist

Breathing	1 min.

Imaginary Journey

Routine 2

Breathe	30 sec.

Neck Stretches
(Up/down, side to side, ear to shoulder)
Seated Reach For the Stars
Seated Half Moon
Seated Cat/Cow
Seated Bicycle
Seated Warrior
Seated Triangle
Seated Lion
Seated Rag Doll
Seated Peanut Butter & Jelly

Breathing	1 min.

Imaginary Journey

Routine 3

Breathe	30 sec.

Standing Reach For the Stars
Standing Rag Doll
Squat – palms together
Grow like a flower
Standing Triangle
Standing Warrior
Seated Frog
Seated Windmill

Breathing	1 min.

Imaginary Journey

Routine 4

Breathe	30 sec.

Floor Exercises
Cat
Horse
Cow
Cobra
Dog
Pigeon
Butterfly
Diamond
Peanut Butter & Jelly

Breathing	1 min.

Imaginary Journey

CHAPTER 2 - WORKSHEET

DIRECTIONS – Associate each week's feeling word with a mindful movement posture. Sit in a circle. Ask students the following questions and allow them to act out their answers. You may need to discuss various feeling words for meaning.

1. When you are angry, would you rather roar like a lion? Purr like a cat? Hiss like a snake?

2. When you are sad, would you rather sleep like a baby? Bend like the moon? Flutter like a butterfly?

3. When you are scared, would you rather curl up like a potato bug? Charge like a warrior? Bark like a dog?

4. When you feel compassionate, would you rather hop like a frog? Ring like a bell? Burn like a candle?

5. When you feel jealous, would you rather stand like a cobra? Erupt like a volcano? Stand erect like a fierce cat?

6. When you feel happy, would you rather stand like a triangle? Pose like a flamingo? Flutter like a butterfly?

7. When you feel anxious, would you rather strut like a pigeon? Moo like a cow? Tower like a tree?

8. When you feel frustrated, would you rather stand like a mountain? Roar like a lion? Mosey like a horse?

9. When you feel guilty, would you rather scurry like a sea crab? Curl up like a potato bug? Hop like a frog?

10. When you feel hurt, would you rather sleep like a child? Fold up like a fan? Curl up like a potato bug?

11. When you feel mischievous, would you rather act like a cat? Slither like a cobra? Sparkle like a diamond?

12. When you feel puzzled, would you rather lie down like sleeping beauty? Bend like the moon? Walk like a crab?

13. When you feel relieved, would you rather shine like a bell? Relax like a pigeon, stretch like a dog?

14. When you feel satisfied, would you rather whinny like a horse? Balance like a tree? Burn like a candle?

15. When you feel disappointed, would you rather fold up like a fan? Curl up like a potato bug? Rest like sleeping beauty?

16. When you feel exhausted, would you rather rest like sleeping beauty, sleep like a child? Fold up like a fan?

CHAPTER 3- WORKSHEET

DIRECTIONS: Fill in the blank with a word from the list of adjectives.
Variation: Read these sentences out loud and have children answer. You can have them each pick one and draw picture showing how they feel.

List of Adjectives:
aggressive, agonized, anxious, apologetic, bashful, blissful, bored, cautious, confident, determined, disappointed, disgusted, ecstatic, enraged, envious, exasperated, exhausted, frightened, frustrated, guilty, happy, horrified, hurt, idiotic, jealous, lonely, mischievous, miserable, optimistic, perplexed, puzzled, regretful, relieved, sad, joyful, satisfied, thoughtful.

1. I feel _____ when I give my opinion and nobody agrees with me.
2. I feel _____ when I ride a roller coaster.
3. I feel _____ when I do my chores.
4. I feel _____ when I'm singing.
5. I feel _____ when I have a lot to do in a short time.
6. I feel _____ when I talk in front of a lot of people.
7. I feel _____ when I eat the last cookie.
8. I feel _____ when I hurt someone's feelings.
9. I feel _____ when I finish my homework.
10. I feel _____ when my best friend pays attention to someone else.
11. I feel _____ when I cross a busy street.
12. I feel _____ when I have trouble solving a problem.
13. I feel _____ when my favorite team wins.
14. I feel _____ when I can't find something I've lost.
15. I feel _____ when someone calls me a name.
16. I feel _____ when I have a cold.
17. I feel _____ after running in a race.
18. I feel _____ when I'm not sure how to respond in a situation.
19. I feel _____ when I compete in an activity.
20. I feel _____ when the sun is shining.

CHAPTER 4- WORKSHEET

DIRECTIONS: Create your own imaginary journey. Think of a place where you feel safe and write about it like you are telling a story.

DIRECTIONS: Create your own imaginary journey. Think of a place where you feel safe and draw a picture of it.

CHAPTER 4- WORKSHEET

CHAPTER 5 WORKSHEETS

DIRECTIONS: Read the feeling words out loud. Allow students to get into postures as a way to express how they feel. Explain the connection between the feeling and the way they hold the energy in their body.

A. Angry

B. Sad

C. Happy

D. Silly

E. Mean

F. Thoughtful

G. Nervous

H. Sorry

I. Shy

J. Confident

K. Disappointed

L. Envious

M. Frightened

N. Lonely

O. Mischievous

P. Confused

Q. Frustrated

R. Relieved

S. Excited

T. Grumpy

SCRIPT FORMAT

Narrator: TWO FRIENDS, LISA AND JODY, WERE SITTING IN CLASS TAKING A TEST. JODY WHO USUALLY DOES WELL, HADN'T STUDIED. JODY DIDN'T KNOW THE ANSWER TO SOME QUESTIONS SO SHE LOOKED AT LISA'S TEST TO GET THE ANSWERS. WHEN TIME WAS UP THE TEACHER COLLECTED THE TESTS. THE TEACHER ASKED LISA AND JODY TO STAY AFTER CLASS THE NEXT DAY.

Teacher: "WILL YOU PLEASE STAY AFTER CLASS?"

Narrator: HE PULLED THEIR TESTS OUT.

Teacher: "YOUR ANSWERS ARE IDENTICAL, I WAS WONDERING IF ONE OF YOU HAS BEEN CHEATING?"

Narrator: JODY HAD ALWAYS DONE WELL IN THE PAST. BOTH GIRLS DENIED CHEATING SO HE BELIEVED JODY WAS TELLING THE TRUTH. HE PUNISHED LISA. LISA WAS ANGRY AND CONFRONTED JODY.

Lisa: "DID YOU COPY OFF ME?"

Narrator: JODY ADMITTED SHE DID CHEAT BUT WAS AFRAID TO TELL THE TRUTH.

The Three Billy Goats Gruff

Once upon a time there were three Billy Goats named Gruff. They lived in a valley with very little food. They needed to go up the hillside to a fine meadow full of grass where they could eat and eat. But on the way they had to pass over a bridge and under the bridge lived an ugly, mean troll. The first Billy Goat passes the bridge. "Trip, Trap, Trip, Trap." "Who's that tripping over my bridge?" "It is I the tiniest Billy Goat." "I'm going to gobble you up," growls the troll. "Oh no, I'm to little that I am. Wait for my brother, he is bigger and will make a better meal." "Well, then, be off with you!" roared the Troll. Off went the little goat. Along came the second Billy Goat, "Trip, Trap, Trip, Trap." "Who's that tripping over my bridge?" roared the Troll. "It is I the second Billy Goat." "I'm going to gobble you up," roared the Troll. "Wait for my brother the 3rd Billy Goat, he is much bigger than I. He will make you a fine meal." "Well, then, be off with you," growled the Troll. Off he went to the meadow. "Trip, Trap, Trip." "Trap, Trip, Trap." Along came the 3rd Billy Goat. "Who's that tripping over my bridge?" roared the Troll. "It is I the 3rd Billy Goat!" and he was as loud as the Troll. "I'm coming to gobble you up," roared the troll. The 3rd goat was not afraid. "Come on up, I have two hard horns and four hard hooves, see what you can do." The troll climbed up the bridge. When he got to the top he was met by the 3rd Billy Goat who quickly butted him into the rushing river. The 3rd Billy Goat continued over the bridge to meet his brothers in the meadow where they ate and ate. They are probably there yet. The End.

CHAPTER 6- WORKSHEET

DIRECTIONS: Think of an animal that is exciting or interesting to you. Imagine how he uses his body to move. Draw a picture of the animal. Write about how it uses its body parts and the overall feeling you get when you think about that animal. Pre-school may act out being the animal.

For example: A bird uses his wings to fly in the sky. He uses his beak as a tool to build nests and eat his food. He uses his feet to grasp a branch. A feeling associated with the bird may be freedom.

Teacher Information Form

Student ID # _____

1. The student has problems controlling behavioral outbursts.
Strongly Agree   Agree   Neutral   Disagree   Strongly Disagree

2. The student has difficulty concentrating in classroom situations.
Strongly Agree   Agree   Neutral   Disagree   Strongly Disagree

3. The student has difficulty interacting with others due to behavior.
Strongly Agree   Agree   Neutral   Disagree   Strongly Disagree

4. The student has difficulty controlling aggression and anger.
Strongly Agree   Agree   Neutral   Disagree   Strongly Disagree

5. The student has poor class attendance due to behavior problems.
Strongly Agree   Agree   Neutral   Disagree   Strongly Disagree

6. The student affects others performance due to behavior problems.
Strongly Agree   Agree   Neutral   Disagree   Strongly Disagree

7. The student's parents are informed of behavior problems regularly.
Strongly Agree   Agree   Neutral   Disagree   Strongly Disagree

8. The student's academic performance has improved with the Rainbow Play program being taught.
Strongly Agree   Agree   Neutral   Disagree   Strongly Disagree

9. The student's behavioral performance has improved with the Rainbow Play program being taught.
Strongly Agree   Agree   Neutral   Disagree   Strongly Disagree

10. As the instructor of this student I feel that the Rainbow Play program is helping the student improve overall.
Strongly Agree   Agree   Neutral   Disagree   Strongly Disagree

DIRECTIONS: Draw a line from the picture to the feeling word that best describes it.

131

Student Information Form

Student ID # _____

Please complete this form to the best of your ability. Answer each statement by circling the best answer that is provided. If you have any questions, please ask your instructor.

1. When I feel pressure in class, I am able to control my behavior.
    Always   Sometimes   Don't feel Pressure   Not Often   Never

2. When I have to take a test, I am able to focus completely on the test.
    Always   Sometimes   Don't Know   Not Often   Never

3. When other people are arguing, like my parents or friends, I can stay calm.
    Always   Sometimes   Don't Know   Not Often   Never

4. When a friend yells or pushes me, I can control my behavior.
    Always   Sometimes   Don't Know   Not Often   Never

5. When I get angry with someone, I can control my behavior.
    Always   Sometimes   Don't Know   Not Often   Never

6. When I am in class, I can control my behavior and not get into trouble.
    Always   Sometimes   Don't Know   Not Often   Never

7. When I am at home, I can control my behavior and not get into trouble.
    Always   Sometimes   Don't Know   Not Often   Never

8. After doing the breathing exercises, I feel good.
    Always   Sometimes   Don't Know   Not Often   Never

9. When I am feeling angry or I am going to lose control, I use my breathing exercises.
    Always   Sometimes   Don't Know   Not Often   Never

10. When I am in class, like reading, I use my breathing exercises to help me concentrate.
    Always   Sometimes   Don't Know   Not Often   Never

Suggested Materials as Reference for Lessons

Preview the materials before integrating them into your lesson. Only use sections that pertain to the lesson.

Books about Feelings

Exploring Emotions Series by Althea - 6 books

Dealing with Feelings Series by Elizabeth Crary - 6 books

Thoughts and Feelings Series by Susan Riley - 12 books

A to Z Do You Ever Feel Like Me? by Bonnie Hausman

Glad Monster/Sad Monster by Ed Emberley and Anne Miranda

My Many Colored Days by Dr. Seuss

Today I Feel Silly and other Moods That Make My Day by Jamie Lee Curtis

Picture Books

Follow Carl by Alexandra Day

Time Flies by Eric Rohmann

Naughty Nancy by John S. Goodall

Frog Goes to Dinner by Mercer Mayer

From Head to Toe by Eric Carle

Animal Alphabet by Bert Kitchen

A Children's Zoo by Tana Hoban

Videos - Nature

See How They Grow Series, Dorling Kindersley Vision

Zoo Life Series, Time Life Video

Eyewitness Series, Dorling Kindersley Vision

Videos - Dance

Hula For Children, Island Heritage

Kidsteps Series, Kidsteps Productions, Inc.

Audio

Mozart Effect, Volumes 1,2,3, Children's Group, Inc.

Hap Palmer's Quiet Places, Hap-Pal Music Inc.

Kevin Kern in the Enchanted Garden, Real Music

Adagio Music For Yoga, Peter Davison, Healing Arts Publishing

Music For A Pipedream, Garry Kvistad & Vinnie Martucci, The Relaxation Company

Merlin's Magic, Reiki, The Light Touch, Inner World Music

Sound of Feelings Music for Exploring Emotions, Jessie Allen Cooper, Cooper Sound Waves

All Time Favorite Dances, Kimbo Educational

Toddlers Sing Rock -n- Roll, Music For Little People

Rock 'n Roll Fitness Fun, Kimbo Educational

Fantasy Kids Classics, EMI Records Ltd.

Additional Sources

Children's Book of Yoga by Thia Luby

Yoga Kids Video, Dancing Feet Yoga Center; Arts & TM Books & Video

The Complete Idiot's Guide to Yoga with Kids by Jodi B. Komitor, M.S., and Eve Adamson

Fly Like a Butterfly by Shakta Kaur Khalsa

Crafts

Paper Animal Masks From Northwest Tribal Tales by Nancy Lyn Rudolph

The Usborne Big Book of Papercraft by Usborne Publishing Ltd.

Look What You Can Make with Paper Bags Edited by Judy Burke

Play with Paper by Sara Lynn and Dianne James

Animal Crafts by Iain MacLeod-Brudenell

Crafty Masks by Thomasina Smith

Simple Puppets From Everyday Materials by Barbara MacDonald Buetter

Crafty Puppets by Thomaina Smith

RESOURCES

Books - Stress Management

Anderson, Bob, (1980). Stretching, California: Shelter Publications.

Carrico, Mara, (1997). Yoga Basics, New York: Henry Holt.

Carroll, Lee & Tober, Jan. (1999) The Indigo Children, CA: Hay House, Inc.

Chopra, M.D., Deepak, (1991) Unconditional Life, Mastering the Forces that Shape Personal Reality, New York: Bantam Books.

Davis, Laura & Keyser, Janis. (1997) Becoming the Parent You Want to Be, New York: Broadway Books.

Deep, Sam & Sussman, Lyle. (1996) Yes, You Can! MA: Addison-Wesley Books.

Evans, Mark. (1999) Instant Message, Oxford: Sebastian Kelly.

Goldstein, Nikki. (1997) Essential Energy, New York: Warner Treasures.

Hay, L. Louise. (1984) You Can Heal Your Life, CA: Hay House, Inc.

Hittleman, Richard. (1969) Yoga 28 Day Exercise Plan, New York: Bantam Books.

Jollands, Beverley. (1999) Instant Calm, Oxford: Sebastian Kelly.

Kabat-Zinn, Ph.D., Jon. (1990) Full Catastrophe Living, New York: Delacorte Press.

Kripalu Center. (1990) Kripalu Yoga Posture Sheets, MA: Kripalu Center.

Lama, The Dalai. (1997) Healing Anger, New York: Snow Lion Publications.

LeShan, Lawrence. (1974) How to Meditate, New York: Bantam Books.

Luby Thia. (1998) Children's Book of Yoga, New Mexico: Clear Light Publishers.

Neuman, Ph.D., Stephanie. (1984) Feelings Everybody Has Them, Ohio: SNB Publishing, Inc.

Pierce, Margaret D. & Pierce, Martin G. (1996) Yoga for Your Life, Oregon: Rudra Press.

Petter, Arjava Frank, (1998) Reiki the Legacy of Dr. Usui, Twin Lakes, WI: Lotus Light Publications.

Parr, Price Penny & Price, Shirley. (1996) Aromatherapy for Babies and Children, London: Thorsons.

Rinpoche, Sogyal. (1992) The Tibetan Book of Living and Dying, New York: Harper Collins.

Verner-Bonds, Lillian. (1999) Colour Healing, London: Lorenz Book.

Books - Educational Drama

Brown, Corinne. (1929) Creative Drama in the Lower School, New York: D. Appleton and Company.

Courtney, Richard. (1995) Drama and Feeling, Canada: McGill-Queen's University Press.

Durland, Frances Caldwell. (1952) Creative Dramatics for Children, U.S.: Kent State University Press.

Erion, Polly. (1997) Drama in the Classroom, California: Lost Coast Press.

Heinig-Beall, Ruth & Stillwell, Lyda. (1974) Creative Drama for the Classroom Teacher, New Jersey: Prentice Hall.

Wagner, Betty Jane. (1999) Building Moral Communities Through Educational Drama, Conneticut: Ablex Publishing Corp.

BOOKS - Educational Philosophy

Gardner, Howard. (1983) Frames of Mind, New York: Harper Collins Publishers, Inc.

Montessori, Maria. (1967) The Absorbent Mind, New York: Holt, Rinehart and Winston.

Video

Wenig, Marsha. (1996) *Yoga Kids*, Michigan: Arts & TM Books & Video.

Audio

Ornish, M.D., Dean. (1998) *The Healing Power of Love and Intimacy*, Co.: Kikim Media.

Articles

De Zengotita, T. (1999) *The Gunfire Dialogues. Harper's Magazine*, v299 (il790), 55.

Conway, C. & Clennell, (1994) *Posturing for Inner Peace. L. Psychology Today*, v27 (n4), 50 -57.

Wenig, M. (1991) *Yoga for Kids.* Yoga Journal, 61.

Internet Resources (March 3, 2000) WWW.NSSC1.ORG, The In-House Report of the National School Safety Center.

Copyright © 2000, 2002, 2003, 2004 Rainbow Play.   All rights reserved.

www.ingramcontent.com/pod-product-compliance
Lightning Source LLC
Chambersburg PA
CBHW080738230426
43665CB00020B/2777